MURDER IN TANDEM

when two people kill

MURDER IN TANDEM

when two people kill

Paul Wilson
James Wulf Simmonds

HarperCollinsPublishers

HarperCollins*Publishers*

First published in Australia in 2000
by HarperCollins*Publishers* Pty Ltd
ABN 36 009 913 517
A member of the HarperCollins*Publishers* (Australia) Pty Limited Group
http://www.harpercollins.com.au

Copyright © Paul Wilson and James Wulf Simmonds 2000

This book is copyright.
Apart from any fair dealing for the purposes of private study, research, criticism or review, as permitted under the Copyright Act, no part may be reproduced by any process without prior written permission.
Inquiries should be addressed to the publishers.

HarperCollins*Publishers*
25 Ryde Road, Pymble, Sydney NSW 2073, Australia
31 View Road, Glenfield, Auckland 10, New Zealand
77–85 Fulham Palace Road, London W6 8JB, United Kingdom
Hazelton Lanes, 55 Avenue Road, Suite 2900, Toronto, Ontario M5R 3L2
and 1995 Markham Road, Scarborough, Ontario M1B 5M8, Canada
10 East 53rd Street, New York NY 10022, USA

National Library of Australia Cataloguing-in-Publication data:

Wilson, Paul R. (Paul Richard), 1941- .
  Murder in tandem: when two people kill.
  Bibliography.
  ISBN 978-0-7322-6936-4.
  1. Murder – Australia – Case Studies.
  2. Murderers – Australia – Case Studies.
  I. Simmonds, James Wulf. II. Title.
364.15230994

Contents

Acknowledgements	6
Preface — When Two People Kill	8
1. A Classic Thrill Killing — Lowery and King	31
2. The Killing of Virginia Morse — Crump and Baker	52
3. The Truro Murders — Miller and Worrell	71
4. Soldiers of Death — Reid and Luckman	89
5. Killing for Love — The Birnies	109
6. Murder for Lust — Watt and Beck	128
7. Opportunity Killing — The Fernando Cousins	143
8. The Sins of the Father — Waters and Cooper	153
9. The Extortionists — Stuart and Finch	162
10. Killing for Business — Peckman and Peckman	177
11. Killing in the Underworld — Wright and Haigh	190
Conclusion — Catching Tandem Killers	203
Bibliography	214

Acknowledgements

Tandem killings have fascinated both of us for many years. In conversations between ourselves we have often asked each other 'What drives people to kill in pairs?'. The related question, of course, is 'Does one of the killers dominate the other and force him or her to commit murder?'. Although some overseas authors have attempted to answer these questions, virtually nothing has been written about Australian tandem murders and the interpersonal dynamics behind them.

One of us, Jim Simmonds, has been a crime journalist for many years while the other, Paul Wilson, is an academic criminologist. Although our differing backgrounds mean we tend to look at crime in different ways, we discovered that we also held in common some basic beliefs about both the characteristics and the causes of tandem killings.

This book is not meant to be an academic thesis on murder nor is it just a journalistic account of gory crimes. We have deliberately aimed for the middle ground and directed both the style of writing and the analysis towards the intelligent layperson. It is for the readers, of course, to decide whether we have achieved our aims.

That this book has been published is thanks to the efforts of several people who have given us valuable help

ACKNOWLEDGEMENTS

and encouragement. Our very special thanks go to Brett Hartley who tirelessly assisted with extensive research and actually prepared early drafts of some chapters. Brett's assistance saved us a great deal of time and helped us to refine our direction. Several other colleagues in the media and academia provided us with material or help in locating it. They know who they are and we thank them, too.

Our sincere appreciation goes to our editors at HarperCollins*Publishers* for their constructive criticism and their professional approach. Special thanks also to Robyn Lincoln, who prepared the manuscript for submission and gave constructive feedback on the early drafts. Her general assistance was crucial in completing this book.

Finally, but importantly, our thanks to our agent, Patricia Lake, for her belief in us and in our work.

Preface

When Two People Kill

There can be no more intimate moment to share with another person than the moment of death. This feeling of ultimate intimacy has been chronicled by sociologists, philosophers, poets and psychopathic killers. In this book we are not concerned with those who share the final moments of a dying loved one, the soldier in battle who grasps the body of a wounded comrade to comfort him as the last vestiges of life seep away, or accidental deaths. Instead we look at those among us who, in the company of another, deliberately and callously take the life of a fellow human being, either as an act of greed or revenge, or because they obtain intense pleasure from committing such deeds.

Motives for murder are always mixed. Though the taboo against killing is strong in the minds of most people, when we examine the background and behaviour of individual murderers, we find that people have a wide variety of reasons for killing someone else. These motives and thought patterns become even more complex when two people act together to commit the most heinous of all crimes.

The personal and social factors associated with homicide and similar violent crimes have been carefully documented by criminologists and other commentators. The problem with many of the classification systems created by them is that such schemes are singularly inept at explaining the intents and purposes of the killers. An exception is the typology adopted by Dr Edward Green in his book *The Intent to Kill: Making Sense of Murder*. In his attempt to identify the most common types of killers, Green distinguishes five categories of murder: predatory, defensive, professional, moral and, finally, what he calls hedonic or hedonistic.

Each of these categories requires some brief explanation. To begin with, predatory murders are those carried out for material gain, such as a murder committed during a bank robbery. The second category, defensive killings, essentially happen as a reaction to some perceived threat either to a person's self-esteem or to their bodily safety, for example, during a pub fight. Under the third category, the professional murderer is, as the label suggests, a person who carries out contract killings without any emotional investment in the death of the victims. On the other hand, the fourth category, moral murderers, often have a strong ideological or emotional belief in the virtue of their actions, such as we see with political terrorists or government-sanctioned genocidal 'goon squads'.

Even though these four patterns are found among both murderers who operate alone and those who act in tandem with another perpetrator, it is the fifth category, the hedonistic killer, that will most concern us in this book. These are the killers who take the life of another for excitement or pleasure. They engage in the act of violence for the thrill of the hunt, for sexual or erotic pleasure, or for the sheer adrenalin rush that comes with the almost God-like feeling of dominating, and then eliminating, another human being.

Serial killers are undoubtedly the archetypal criminal in this category. These killers have been the subject of countless films and books as well as academic analyses. While it is not our intention to repeat what has been said about such offenders, it is clear that many tandem killers obtain the same almost sensual experience of intimacy in killing another human that was so apparent in the motives of men like Ted Bundy or Jeffrey Dahmer. Among America's most infamous serial killers, Bundy murdered as many as forty young women and Dahmer preyed mainly on adolescent males, killing and dismembering them. But comparing the hedonistic pleasures of lone serial killers with those who murder in tandem raises some questions: for example, is the intimacy of a killer sharing the final moment of a victim's life doubled or halved when mutually carried out with an accomplice? And, given that for most people one of the greatest deterrents to violence is for their actions to become known to others, what brings two people together to the point where they plan together and encourage each other to commit murder?

As we shall see in the cases we examine, a comparison between tandem murderers and those who act alone also raises issues relating to the female killer. Women have always committed fewer murders than men and explanations for this are varied. One common view is that although women have as many opportunities as men to commit murder and are inherently as criminal, the role society places on them as women directs most female crime into non-violent offences such as social security fraud, prostitution and shoplifting.

Some feminists, such as American criminologist Freda Adler, argue that female crime rates will rise to match male rates as views about acceptable female roles and behaviour become less rigid and constrained. Nonetheless, crime statistics show that while female offending has increased in general in recent years, their involvement in violent offences, especially murder, is still minimal. Females who commit defensive murder often do so because they have suffered brutal victimisation at the hands of their partners. Only recently have courts recognised that there is a breaking point that a woman may reach after years of abuse. Then, in a moment of fear and deep hatred, she may erupt into committing a spontaneous act of violence against her male partner.

There are other forms of murder committed by women but they are relatively rare. For example, female serial killers most certainly exist as the infamous case of Aileen Wuornos in Florida in 1992 demonstrates. In this well-publicised case the killer approached motorists for help, claiming that her car had broken down. Often she would offer sex as a reward for assistance. She then shot them, taking their wallets as they lay dead or dying. Though women murderers and serial offenders have killed for money (as in cases where they murder their husbands or partners for insurance purposes) or in other situations (such as killing babies or old people under their care) there are few examples of lone female multiple murderers who engage in violence for erotic or sensual reasons. The exception to this rule, it would appear, is in the case of female hedonistic tandem killers such as the infamous Moors murderer Myra Hindley. Hindley, who is serving a life sentence in Highpoint prison, Suffolk, UK, along with her partner Ian Brady, also serving life in gaol, was convicted in 1966 of a series of child murders. The pair tortured their victims while recording their screams and sobs on tape, before killing them and burying their bodies on the Yorkshire Moors.

In some of the chapters that follow we will examine Australian cases where a man, apparently with the full support of his female partner, engages in brutal and horrendous violence seemingly for purely hedonistic reasons. But before turning to the Australian cases, let us briefly look at some famous British and American examples of tandem killing. Some of the overseas cases are legendary and include Rosemary and Fred West of the United Kingdom 'House of Horrors' case; and the Moors murderers, Ian Brady and Myra Hindley. In Australia equivalent killers include Catherine and David Birnie, and Barrie Watt and Valmae Beck. Later in this book we will discuss the motivation for the woman's role in these killings in more detail. At this stage, however, it is relevant to mention that a common explanation for these relationships is based on the concept of dominance.

A dominance explanation of tandem killing suggests that a controlling, highly sexed male emotionally exploits a more submissive and emotionally fragile female. One classic example of this relationship can be seen in the much-publicised American 'sex slave' case where a husband and wife team, Gerald and Charlene Gallego, kidnapped and murdered at least seven young women. Gerald Gallego had an intense fantasy life that revolved around his desire for the 'perfect sex slave' — preferably an adolescent virgin — who he could hold captive and submit to every known sexual act. Together with Charlene, Gerald was able to put into practice a plan of abduction whereby young girls were forced into his van, sexually tormented and finally executed. When arrested Charlene was initially reluctant to give evidence against her husband but was eventually persuaded to enter a plea bargain that required her to testify against Gerald. In interviews with detectives the young woman explained her involvement in the killings on the ground that she required the emotional security that her husband provided and her price for this security was to help him play out his ultimate 'sex slave' fantasy.

Similar explanations for a woman's involvement in tandem killings are given in other popular or academic accounts of such crimes. When, in October 1995, Rosemary West, the wife of the British multiple killer

Fred West, was herself tried and eventually convicted of serial murder, both the media and the public were appalled. How, it was asked, could such a quiet, apparently family-oriented woman willingly engage in some of the most grotesque and horrible acts of violence in British criminal history? This was the woman who saved the sperm of her lovers and then injected it into her daughters; this was the woman who enjoyed watching her husband slowly strangling to death his young victims and then committed the same crime herself; this was the woman who helped fit a mask onto a rope-bound female so that a plastic tube curled upwards from the mouth into the nostrils — a device designed to prolong the victim's life so the killers could extend their enjoyment of the perverted pleasures of sexual torture.

Psychologist Paul Britton, who worked with the police on the West case, stated that Fred and Rosemary 'were both involved and were equal partners — they didn't just kill for the sake of taking a life: their victims were playthings who were tortured and abused' (*The Australian*, 27 November 1995). Equal partners, perhaps, but equally responsible for the ghastly crimes they committed? Not so, says British writer Brian Masters, author of *She Must Have Known*, a fascinating analysis of the twelve murders committed by Fred and Rosemary West. Masters advances the argument that when a woman and a man are involved in tandem killing, the woman has usually been systematically drawn by the man into his web of murder and violence. He is the dominant one and she the submissive partner, not in control of herself and acting almost as an automaton.

Thus, in explaining Rosemary West's involvement in the horrendous murders, Masters suggests that Fred West, an evil psychopath, was able to ensnare his wife into a web of unseeing complicity. Rosemary West's 'greatest misfortune was to have been the wife of a psychotic', writes Masters. To be fair to the writer, he does not entirely excuse Rosemary from her crimes. Indeed, he argues that it is entirely possible the woman was depraved and more than just a mere accessory to the series of ghastly crimes. But in the final analysis the thesis advanced by Masters is that Rosemary was a woman of low self-esteem who fell victim to a sexual sadist, a man who subjected her to a systematic and escalating regime of physical and psychological abuse. Masters contends that Rosemary was a long-term victim of her dominant husband, and not a 'free agent' as decided by the jury which convicted her of murder.

Masters argues forcibly that in most of the cases involving murder for pleasure by a man and a woman, the female offender has been slowly but systematically socialised into obeying the man. Masters' view is that the male, usually a sadist, exerts control over his female partner in every aspect of her life even though this control may not be readily apparent to those who know the couple. 'There was nothing in Rosemary's past to indicate criminal tendencies,' Masters writes. He suggests that Fred West worked on Rosemary's low self-esteem so that she felt loved and needed by him. Masters' view is that in the West case, and in most other tandem killings involving both sexes, the man systematically works at captivating the female by charm but combines this approach with the threat of leaving the woman if she does not submit to his usually violent sexual fantasies. In this way the female is forced into becoming a willing — and murderous — accomplice.

The implication of this line of reasoning is that the female submissive partner would never be involved in murder if it were not for her involvement with the highly pathological dominant male. This argument is advanced to explain many cases of tandem murder. When commenting on the Birnie case (see Chapter 5), Masters quotes an unnamed psychologist who apparently said that he had never seen anyone so emotionally dependent upon another person as Catherine Birnie had been with David. This analysis does not accord with our own interpretation of the Birnie case or, indeed, of many of the other cases we have examined in this book. Although Catherine Birnie had told her barrister that she had taken part in the killings out of her love for David, she did not display a rigid compliance with every request made by her husband. Indeed, Catherine exhibited streaks of jealousy and even threatened to leave David — threats that made him decide to kill Noelene Patterson even though he was clearly infatuated with her.

The alternative view, rejected by Masters, is that the man and woman feed the other's willingness or desire to kill, whether because of bravado; a willingness to go to extremes out of love or fear; or through the perverse, macabre pleasure of sharing in an act known to be utterly forbidden. Untangling the relative truth of these two contrasting views is one of the aims of this book and we will return to the issue after discussing our Australian examples of tandem killings.

What, though, if the perpetrators are both male? Does the same dominance–submission relationship that so many writers claim exist in these situations? And is there an overt or latent homosexual relationship between the two men? As we will see in the chapters to come, in some such cases the stronger of the pair leads the weaker into murder and frequently forces the latter to commit the crime under some form of duress, but not always. There are many case of two males killing where the weaker of the pair evolves into the most vicious and sadistic perpetrator. Is Masters' explanation of dominance and submission perhaps too simplistic to explain the complex interplay between partners involved in killing for pleasure?

One thing becomes apparent, however, when the dynamics between tandem murderers are explored; it is clear the loyalties in relationships built on murder are particularly fragile. From the point of arrest, one of the duo almost always sells out to the police, claiming no part in the physical act of killing. Alternatively, they suggest that they were forced into it in some way by their partner, and frequently it is the obvious ringleader who most vociferously accuses the weaker partner of being the stronger influence in the crime or crimes. Oddly, despite recrimination and counter-recrimination throughout interview, committal and trial procedures, some murdering couples appear to resurrect their friendship at a later stage, either in gaol or on release.

In many of the other cases we have examined it is difficult for us to accept that the more submissive killer committed crimes because he or she was so dominated by the other. Paul Luckman (Chapter 4) may well have been a great deal younger and less experienced than his partner-in-crime Robin Reid, but he willingly engaged in their mutual fantasies of torture and murder, and appeared to enjoy the violence inflicted upon their victim, Peter Aston. And, as the trial judge noted, Luckman appeared to make no attempt to escape from Reid or to stop him from committing the horrible violence suffered by Aston.

In most of the Australian cases that we have examined there does not appear to be evidence to support the proposition that in hedonistic tandem murder there is necessarily a leader–follower situation where the follower is intellectually and morally weaker than the leader and therefore inextricably forced into murder. Though there may be a dominant personality among couples who kill, this does not necessarily imply that the less dominant person wished to refrain from the violence. This was the case with Watt and Beck (Chapter 6), Lowery and King (Chapter 1) and Crump and Baker (Chapter 2) and, indeed, with most of the other cases we investigated.

Perhaps the closest Australian case approximating the Brian Masters' thesis is that of Miller and Worrell (Chapter 3). Miller was sexually attracted to Worrell although these feelings did not appear to be strongly reciprocated. And, while Worrell committed most of the actual killings, Miller knew what Worrell was doing and did not try to stop any of the murders, even though he probably could have. Miller's excuse, that he was under threat from Worrell, rings hollow when you take into consideration the multiple opportunities that were available to him to escape from Worrell or at least to inform the police and gain their protection.

We do not deny that under some circumstances a dominance–submission relationship may exist where the submissive partner is almost forced to commit crimes by the sheer superiority of will that one person exerts over the other. Masters is probably correct when he suggests that this influence is more likely to exist when a relationship between two partners occurs in an atmosphere of intense secrecy and isolation, with minimal contact with friends or, in the case of a married couple, other relatives. Some well-known American and English cases illustrate this pattern and give insight into the complex, ever-changing relationship of dominance–submission relationships that exist between at least some tandem killers.

In the Hillside Strangler killings in the US, Kenneth Bianchi was essentially a weak-willed person who'd always wanted to be 'somebody' in life but never was.

When, as a young adult, he moved in to live with his cousin, Angelo Buono, he was immediately captivated by the older man's success and his material possessions. Buono had his own car-body repair shop and a well-furnished flat. What most impressed Bianchi, however, was his cousin's ability to obtain young teenagers as lovers and to get them to perform oral sex with him. Bianchi became fascinated by the endless sexual possibilities that a life with Buono offered. As a result of their association, at least ten young girls were murdered and their naked bodies dumped on hillsides in the Los Angeles area. Most of the young women had been strangled or stabbed to death and sexually assaulted either vaginally or anally.

As often happens in the relationship between tandem killers, however, the dominant partner became bored with the more submissive partner. In the case of Buono, he asked Bianchi to move out of his apartment and to live alone. When Bianchi was held by the police in another state as a possible suspect for other murders, the link between the two men began to unravel. Bianchi wrote to his cousin to reassure him that he would never inform the police about Buono's involvement. Buono made the fatal mistake of phoning Bianchi and hinting that if he ever weakened in his resolve not to involve Buono, then Buono would extract vengeance by murdering members of Bianchi's family. From that moment on, Bianchi turned hero worship into overt hostility for Buono. He forgot about protecting Buono and decided to devote his energies to saving his own skin. After complex and dramatic separate trials, the two men were eventually found guilty of multiple murders and sentenced to life imprisonment. Though Bianchi never gave direct evidence against his cousin, it was apparent that he was more concerned with his own position than in helping his once dominant partner in crime.

The same pattern of dominance and submission was probably at work in the case of the two Moors murderers. Myra Hindley described her lover, Ian Brady, as being 'marvellously exciting' and was captivated by Brady's obsessive interest in Nazis, the ideas of the Marquis de Sade and his interest in committing the perfect murder. Brady appeared to be able to lead Hindley into participating in sadistic acts that she would not otherwise have contemplated.

As with most of our Australian cases, however, this is not to say that the less dominant person, in this case Hindley, was simply a passive follower of Brady's violent fantasies. Indeed, in the first murder they committed Hindley used her van to pick up a girl that she said Brady eventually raped and murdered. Brady, however, in an open letter to the British media, contradicted Hindley's account of the killing, saying that at least some of the wounds inflicted on the sixteen-year-old girl were delivered by Hindley. In fact Brady accused Hindley of strangling Lesley Ann Downey, another of their victims, 'with her own hands'. Although Hindley has denied her active participation in any of the murders committed by the pair, it is very clear that, though infatuated with Brady, Myra Hindley was a willing and committed partner in the Moors murders.

As we have seen, wives, girlfriends and homosexual lovers of dominant males are frequently found to be active participants in tandem violence. One of the first documented American cases illustrating this pattern involved the rape of a fourteen-year-old girl in 1963 by Lloyd Higdon and his wife in Lansing, Michigan. The victim was given a ride by the couple and then raped by Higdon in their house, an offence for which Higdon was sentenced to two years imprisonment. After his release Higdon began a new relationship with a twenty-nine-year-old woman. The two of them then picked up a thirteen-year-old girl and drove her to a rubbish dump where she was repeatedly raped by Higdon before he strangled her to death. Although Higdon was found guilty of murder, his girlfriend escaped a murder charge and was convicted instead of abduction. What was interesting in this case, however, was the ability of the dominant man to attract the attention of two submissive women and involve them in grotesque crimes.

Like Myra Hindley, the two women involved in Higdon's crimes would probably not have engaged in such violence if they had not come under the influence of a highly dominant man. Indeed, drawing on the work of the psychologist Abraham Maslow, some observers of crimes committed by couples have argued that many female killers, in particular, actually seek out relationships with males who are more dominant and controlling than they are themselves. Some of Maslow's studies give credence to this view. The psychologist noted that women preferred to be with males who were slightly more dominant than they were themselves. And, as the crime writer Colin Wilson has pointed out, this dominance symbiosis works not only in romantic and sexual relationships but also in many crime partnerships. He further suggests that moderately dominant females are especially likely to fall under the power of highly dominant males.

It may well be that this is what happened in the case of the Birnies and Watt and Beck. Both women were at least 'moderately dominant' and it could be argued that David Birnie and Barrie Watt were highly dominant males. It also appears that in each case the women actively pursued and sought out their partners despite being rebuffed and humiliated by them. But the dominance hypothesis is not only confined to male and female relationships. Indeed, one of the most notorious crime partnerships that has emerged this century is that between Richard Loeb and Nathan Leopold. These two Chicago students from wealthy families committed a murder which apparently had no motive other than the fact that they wanted to see what it was like to commit a murder.

Loeb was the dominant person in their friendship and he obviously enjoyed manipulating and controlling Leopold who, it is clear, revelled in being the object of Loeb's control. Their partnership in crime was very much a master–slave relationship and the self-esteem of

Loeb was 'stroked' by the adoration that the weaker man bestowed on him. But there was more to their life of crime and their personal relationship than just this. The dominant Loeb could obtain some satisfaction from the submissive Leopold but much more was needed to feed his ravenous ego. By committing the ultimate deviant act — the killing of a stranger — and by involving Leopold in the killing, Loeb was able to more fully express his need for self-recognition and dominance. In fact it is doubtful that Leopold would have become involved in such an act of violence if he had not willingly submitted his personality to the control of someone else.

Whether the aggressive Loeb needed the submissive Leopold in order to commit a murder is another matter. Would Brady have killed without Hindley or, for that matter, would Fred West have engaged in horrific acts of sexual sadism and murder without his wife? We shall, of course, never know the answer to these questions. Without any doubt, though, the coming together of a dominant person and a less dominant one, combined with a penchant by one or both for particularly violent sexual acts, increases the probability of the pair becoming involved in brutal acts of violence.

It seems likely that the same processes involved in the Loeb–Leopold partnership also apply in a number of our Australian cases. In particular, there appears to have been a great desire on the part of the more dominant partner in the hedonistic killings to involve the weaker, more submissive person in the acts of violence and murder. But where our view differs from that of other analysts is that we do not believe the weaker person was so overwhelmed by the dominant partner that they were compelled to engage in the murders. We doubt, for example, that Baker so confounded Crump that Crump had no choice but to involve himself in the savage rape and murder of Virginia Morse. Likewise, there is little evidence to suggest that Luckman was forced to participate in murder because of Reid's influence, or that one of the Fernando cousins (Chapter 7) so overwhelmed the other that he, too, was compelled to participate in the killing of Sandra Hoare.

We do not deny that some cases of what has been called *folie à deux* do exist. In this situation one person exerts an almost mesmerising power over the other. Although we would not concede that the Wests fall into this category, it is very possible that Leopold and Loeb do, along with two quite well-known New Zealand cases. The first was the 1954 case of Pauline Parker and Juliet Hulme, and the second was the death-by-exorcism drama involving Janice and Lindsay Gibson in 1993. Hulme and Parker were two teenage girls who were involved in a quasi-lesbian friendship that attracted the condemnation of Pauline's parents. Believing that their relationship was under threat they lured Pauline's mother into a Christchurch park and battered her to death with a brick in a stocking.

In the exorcism case, Janice and Lindsay Gibson became swept up in a vortex of powerful, hypermanic religious energy that made them both believe that the devil was infecting their children and the fortunes of the family. A series of what they believed were intrusions by the devil into their children's lives culminated in the attempted exorcism of their twelve-year-old son Dane. Lindsay, who had for some time referred to his wife as 'God' was ordered by Janice to hold the boy down while she engaged in the exorcism. In the process the boy's wrists were broken, although this did not stop Janice continuing the exorcism by taking a broken concrete block and repeatedly hitting her son on the head with it. Alarmed by the child's screams, neighbours alerted the police who found a naked Lindsay in the back yard still holding down the dying boy. The husband did not look at his wife, believing that it was blasphemy to cast ones eyes at 'God'. The two were charged with murder but were found not guilty because they were seen as victims of a psychotic illness known as *folie à deux*, which translates as 'madness shared by two'.

It should be noted that *folie à deux* is a very uncommon disorder which is distinguished from other conditions involving two people engaged in an intense relationship by the presence of psychosis in the dominant person. In most of the cases that we have raised in this chapter — or indeed in this book — there is no suggestion that one of the pairs of killers is psychotic either in a psychiatric or legal sense.

So, if we rule out mutual 'madness' as a cause of tandem killing, what is it that drives tandem killers to murder? The popular excuse is that the killers have been victims of child abuse. Fred West said at one stage that he was such a victim, although Rosemary never used this kind of self-justification. Some of our Australian killers such as Paul Luckman and James Miller argued that they had been badly abused as children, and perhaps they had. But even when killers have suffered abuse as children, it is hard to see why one person who has been sexually abused becomes a killer while another decides to tread a more peaceful path through life. Child abuse in itself is a fairly unsatisfactory explanation of why an individual offender becomes a killer, and it becomes even more unsatisfactory when trying to explain the behaviour of those who murder in pairs.

One important clue to discovering the causes of tandem killings is, however, the way in which each of the killers reacts to their early childhood experiences. Paul Britton compellingly argues that when Fred and Rosemary West were growing up and discovering their sexuality, they did not learn to see other people as separate, unique individuals with their own needs and desires. Indeed, in reconstructing their crimes it becomes apparent that Fred and Rosemary fused the sexual and emotional needs of their victims with their own feelings. At least for Fred, women became sexual objects to be abused, exploited and ultimately killed. The bodies of the young women he murdered became little more than fleshy vessels through which he expressed murderous fantasies — fantasies that he began to develop in childhood and consolidated in adolescence.

Despite the need to exercise caution in blaming 'child abuse' for subsequent sexual murder, it is clear that couples or individuals who engage in sexually sadistic killings have often had a grossly disturbed and pathological childhood. between 1947 and 1950 Raymond Fernandez and Martha Beck swindled and then brutally murdered lonely women seeking partners. It was one of America's first 'couples' serial killings. Known as the 'Lonely Hearts' murderers, both killers had parents who dealt with them savagely and failed to give them emotional support and love.

With infamous lone serial killers — Wayne Gacy and Ted Bundy, for example — we find the same pattern. They also experienced childhoods punctuated by a combination of strict punitive discipline and an absence of normal parental love and attention. This pattern has emerged in an overwhelming number of our Australian cases, and not only those we have defined as 'hedonistic'. For example, in the Wright and Haigh murders (Chapter 11) and the Whiskey Au Go Go case (Chapter 9) the killers all appeared to have experienced an upbringing that was devoid of sustained love and consistent emotional support.

The inherent weakness of tandem murderers appears to be twofold: one, the uncertainty of being able to rely totally on a partner in murder; and two, that in some such cases the victim is known in some way to one or the other of the perpetrators. Both of these elements have helped to bring tandem killers to justice, the second perhaps being more important than the first since the crumbling alliance rarely takes place until police questioning of the suspects begins.

But if there is no connection between the killers and the victims, then the task for the investigator is very difficult indeed. The art (or is it science?) of offender profiling portrayed in numerous films and television dramas may help somewhat but it is hardly a panacea for successfully concluding investigations into these horrific killings. At best, profiling gives the investigators some concept of the type of person or persons they are seeking. While the profile can prove to be startlingly accurate after a perpetrator is arrested, it does not provide hard evidence leading to a successful completion of the investigation.

What generally happens in the solving of tandem killings is that luck plays a major role. Potential victims escape or tandem killers become complacent and leave obvious clues, allowing detectives to catch the murderers. This element of luck is often compounded by the extraordinary advances made in recent years in forensic science, enabling investigators to extract hard evidence from crime scene trace material.

Lest it be thought that all tandem murders revolve around hedonistic motives, we have deliberately included three examples of killings motivated for basically predatory reasons. We have relied on court transcripts and newspaper accounts to reconstruct the events that we describe in this book. In addition, in some instances we have supplemented these sources with personal interviews either with the killers themselves (as in the Reid–Luckman case) or with police or reporters who investigated or covered the cases (as in Lowery and King, the Birnies, and Crump and Baker). As to the background of the killers, it has not always been possible to obtain the sort of detail we would have liked. Imperfect as our information might be on this point, we were uniformly struck by the pitifully inadequate and depressed family and personal backgrounds of almost all the killers covered in this book. In some such cases — such as the Birnies — we illustrate this background in some detail.

Many people, however, no matter whether they turn to crime or not, have such backgrounds; but few, very few, embark on wanton killing sprees like those we outline in the chapters that follow. In almost every case we write about it appears to us there was always a point at which the killers could have turned away from the violence they subsequently inflicted. A deprived and alienated background offers, perhaps, some explanation for the reasons why individuals turn to horrific violence, but it fails to excuse their actions.

1

A CLASSIC THRILL KILLING

Lowery and King

The hedonistic killer, as we saw in the opening chapter, is someone who takes the life of another for excitement or pleasure. In recent years we've become familiar with the term 'thrill kill' because of its frequent use in the media, but it was unheard of twenty-eight years ago, when rural Australia was easing itself into the 1970s. Country townships still lag behind larger cities in development but, thanks to the miracles of modern electronic communication, by no means as far as they did in 1971 when the nation experienced its first thrill killing — or, at least, the first one dubbed that by the media.

The killing took place on the outskirts of Hamilton, in western Victoria, which had once been the thriving centre of one of Australia's richest grazing districts. In the 1950s the international wool market was booming, creating full employment and making Hamilton a desirable place to live and raise a family. Towards the end of the decade, a decline in wool prices led to a decline in the national economy and Hamilton's growth began to slow. At that time the city had one cinema, which changed its program twice each week, two department stores, a handful of milk bars and four pubs.

Regular entertainment for the city's youth was restricted to the movies, a Saturday night dance, football club pie nights, a local basketball league and church groups such as the Anglican 'Younger Set'. The favourite practice of red-blooded young males was to spend their evenings driving their cars — mostly Holdens or Fords — up and down the main street looking for some 'action'. In most cases, these patrols could have been described as 'search and destroy missions', because the young men's search for females willing to participate in the remainder of the evening was almost always fruitless, leading to a destruction of their fragile, developing male egos.

Frequently, after the usual Gray Street prowl had ended in disappointment, two or three carloads of youths would contribute towards 'a dozen' of beer — this was in the days before 'stubbies' became common. Once they were equipped with sufficient grog, the youths would drive out of town to find an isolated place where they'd get drunk and often fight each other. At other times they'd try to out-race each other using the public highway as a drag strip, occasionally killing themselves and/or other people in horrendous car accidents. This kind of ritual was repeated in small towns and cities throughout Australia. In more recent years, Hamilton and many other rural cities and towns have developed sports centres offering indoor activities such as basketball, volleyball and table tennis, although successive generations of young men still practise the habits of their forebears.

In 1971 little had changed in Hamilton since its boom days of the 1950s, except that money and work were considerably harder to get. From time to time the city had been shaken by scandals, but not many of them made national news. One of the few exceptions was an allegation that a prominent local businessman and city councillor had sold condoms to schoolchildren; of course this was before the AIDS virus had become widely known, and before juvenile sex had become the rule rather than the exception.

Although Hamilton was technically classified as a city by most international standards it was a fairly sleepy Australian country town. It was so far removed from the dangerous milieu of most larger, modern cities that, on Sunday 31 January 1971, fifteen-year-old Rosalyn Mary Nolte saw no peril in taking her corgi dog, Jodie, for an evening walk. Earlier that day Rosalyn had shown her pedigree pet at the Hamilton Dog Show, and she was still wearing an enamel Kennel Club badge on her woollen sweater.

Rosalyn, a pretty girl with shoulder-length dark blonde hair, left her home around 6.15 pm knowing that, at the height of the summer, she had more than two hours of daylight left. Around 8 pm, she and the corgi were walking along Gray Street when a blue Holden panel van drew up beside her. The van was driven by eighteen-year-old

Christopher Russell Lowery. It belonged to his father Bill, a well-known local bricklayer with a reputation for being a good, honest worker and solid family man. Lowery's passenger was Charles Ian King, also eighteen, and also from a well-established local family. As it later turned out, during the Christmas period a month earlier, these two had agreed 'to kill a chick' just to see what it was like. The macabre concept apparently came to them during a weekend of booze and motorcycle racing at Mt Gambier in South Australia, just across the western Victorian border.

While it is always difficult to analyse dispassionately a vicious crime, the killing of Rosalyn by Lowery and King is a graphic example of the forces which writers like Masters suggest come into play in tandem murder, especially when committed by two males. There is evidence here of a dominant partner exercising power over a more submissive partner, and of that more submissive partner striving to show bravado rather than subservience as a means of winning the dominant partner's respect or, at least, acceptance by him as an equal. The challenge, though, is to identify which of the killers was actually dominant. Lowery was married and his wife was pregnant with their first child, but this should not be taken as a sign of maturity on his part. Both men were assessed as being of above-average intelligence, though this is not necessarily an attribute of those who commit tandem killings.

The killers spun Rosalyn a false yarn as a result of which she accepted a ride in the van, taking her dog with her. Lowery drove the van sixteen kilometres out of town before turning onto a bush track leading to Mt Napier Reserve. Earlier in the day the reserve had probably hosted at least some Australia Day weekend picnickers but by the time the trio and dog arrived there, it was deserted enough to count as pretty much the middle of nowhere. Despite its grandiose name, the extinct volcano of Mt Napier is little more than a rock-strewn hill and the reserve was, at that time, untidy scrub rather than the attractive place its name might imply.

Rosalyn's mother, June, forty-two, was to tell police later that her daughter left for a short walk with the corgi; she'd planned to wash her hair when she returned home, in readiness for showing Jodie at the Warrnambool Dog Show the next day. It was twelve hours later, on Monday morning, that police decided to start searching for the missing girl. Hamilton CIB Detective Norm Mengler had been stationed Hamilton city for many years. A bullishly built man, Detective Mengler looked the archetypal tough cop yet was widely respected in Hamilton and known to be a very gentle man by nature. His experience of the district and the scrub country surrounding the town told him that finding Rosalyn without help was close to impossible.

Help came in the form of Jodie, Rosalyn's faithful corgi. The dog had returned home alone, eventually leading police to the vicinity of the missing girl's body. They then followed a trail of discarded clothing to their grisly find. Rosalyn's naked body lay in a hollow at the base of Mt Napier. She had been trussed hand and foot with electrical flex. Veteran police roundsman Seaton Ashton, then known to his colleagues at Melbourne's *Sun News Pictorial* newspaper as 'The King', reported succinctly: 'Rosalyn's body — naked except for a pair of sockettes — was found on Wednesday off a lonely dirt track nine miles south of Hamilton. She had been strangled.'

Experienced police, including some of Victoria's most capable detectives, were sickened by the obvious extent of Rosalyn's suffering. One was to comment: 'This is the work of a deranged person or persons; there is little pattern to the murder.' Even the weather conspired to make the investigation more difficult. Heavy rain had washed the ground around Mt Napier, making it difficult for forensic specialists to find evidence but they did manage to locate some tyre tracks, which would prove vital in the coming trial. The small size of Hamilton helped police to build an account of Rosalyn's last hours. Accompanied by her dog, she had spent some time in an amusement hall on Gray Street with some friends, leaving about 8 pm.

The local grapevine was active. It was all but impossible to be on Gray Street any evening without being seen by someone, and so it was that within twenty-four hours of the discovery of Rosalyn's body, police were said to have conducted 'a routine interview' with a youth in the larger provincial city of Ballarat, and another with a man in Melbourne. Three days later Lowery, an apprentice bricklayer, and King, a shop assistant, were charged with the murder. They appeared in the Hamilton Magistrates' Court on 8 February and were remanded to Melbourne, eventually standing trial in the Supreme Court of Victoria at Ballarat, the city renowned in history as the site of the Eureka Stockade.

Mr Justice Smith presided over the trial. One of the state's most experienced prosecutors, Mr Geoff Byrne, opened the crown case before an all-male jury. Lowery was represented by Mr RJ Davern Wright QC, and King by Mr HC Ogden QC.

Mr Byrne told a hushed court, its public gallery packed, that Lowery and King had murdered Rosalyn simply for the sensation of watching her suffer and die. 'It was one of those murders done for sensation, to see what it would be like to do it,' he said. He told the jury of the fantasy that Lowery and King had decided on at the Mt Gambier motorcycle meeting — namely, to kill a young girl. They had, he said, thought about it and developed the idea. He quoted Lowery as saying: 'It just sort of built up and up and up.' As we will see in other cases in this book, the development of a fantasy of killing someone is a common occurrence in thrill killings.

When Rosalyn responded to their approach on Hamilton's main street, she unwittingly gave them the opportunity to fulfil their plan, Mr Byrne said. He continued: 'The accused men enticed her by fraud and detained her by force. Rosalyn Nolte was driven out in the bush and strangled to death by some ingenious method. Some thought she had been put into a loop around the throat and a slipknot around the back of the neck.' He described how Rosalyn's legs and arms had been tied with two-core electrical flex, a loop of which was passed around her throat then tied to her legs, forcing her body to bend backwards. Rosalyn had been kicked in the face and stomped on the back before her death. She died slowly of asphyxiation as the flex tightened around her throat.

Fingerprints on a beer can, the pattern of tyre tracks from the rear wheels of his panel van matching tracks at the scene, and a clear match between the flex used to bind Rosalyn and flex found in the van tied Lowery to the crime. Throughout the trial each of the accused tried to lay the blame on the other but, since they seemed to be on friendly terms when allowed outside the court under guard for a cigarette, Mr Byrne suggested the blame-shifting was no more than a ploy to try and confuse the jury.

All the evidence, however, suggests that Lowery was the dominant personality and the ringleader, and that King was a more submissive but still more than willing accomplice. In other words, while Lowery was the dominant partner it was never suggested that he slowly and systematically over a period of time directed King into criminal activities that King otherwise would not have been part of. In his confession to police after his arrest, Lowery had said he had held Rosalyn while King undressed her. His memory faltered on some aspects but he recalled that King, before tying her with the flex, tried to rape Rosalyn but failed to penetrate her. Lowery claimed he then told King: 'That will do. Let's go.'

King's recollections, not surprisingly, differed considerably. He remembered Lowery saying it would be good to see Rosalyn struggling as she died. King also said Lowery had kicked her and tried to strangle her with her bra. When Lowery gave evidence, though, he told the court he had been and still was frightened of King. He claimed he was scared for the sake of his pregnant wife because King had threatened her. He said he had picked King up in the panel van shortly after 7.15 pm on the night of the murder. Soon afterwards, King had taken a tablet from an envelope and swallowed it. Lowery said he believed the tablet was the hallucinatory drug LSD. King had told him it was 'acid', and he understood that 'acid' was LSD.

Lowery denied killing Rosalyn or planning to kill a girl. On the night of the murder, he claimed, he and King had seen Rosalyn in Gray Street and she waved to them. 'King asked me if I would stop. I pulled up and she came up to the car,' he said. King then asked Rosalyn whether she knew that a friend named Gary Bailey was back home, and Rosalyn asked them to take her to see him. Lowery said King told her that Bailey would be at a party and Rosalyn asked if they would take her to the party. Under direction from King, Lowery said, he drove to Mt Napier. 'I thought he wanted to have sex with her,' he said.

According to Lowery, at the Mt Napier Reserve King climbed out of the panel van and asked Rosalyn if she wanted to go for a walk. Lowery added: 'They walked off up the track.' He stayed at the van, cleaning inside it and drinking a can of beer. King returned alone to the van and opened the door. 'I asked him if he wanted a beer,' Lowery told the court. 'He looked in the van, saw the flex and said, "No, that will do me". I wondered what he was doing with the flex.'

Lowery claimed that his curiosity led him to follow King because King had shown him 'a few things to do while on LSD' and he thought it might be something like that. He walked sixty or seventy metres until he saw King and Rosalyn. 'I could not see what they were doing and then I could see that he was trying to strangle her. I ran at him and when I got there he brushed me away and knocked me down,' he said.

King, said Lowery, was the one who came up with their alibi tale that they had been driving a hitchhiker to Coleraine, about thirty-five kilometres from Hamilton, at the time they were alleged to have picked up Rosalyn. He also said King had made threats against his wife, who was eight months pregnant when Rosalyn was murdered. Cross-examined by Mr Byrne, Lowery said King had told him the previous September that he had been using drugs, including hashish and marijuana. He told King's counsel Mr Ogden QC, that he had been and still was scared of King. Lowery also denied it had been his idea to 'kill a chick'.

When King came to the witness stand, he presented himself as a distant observer of Rosalyn's murder, seeing her and Lowery through a drug-induced haze. Questioned by Mr Wright for Lowery, he admitted he had once been a member of the Nomads Chapter of the biker gang Hell's Angels. King also admitted owning a book about the US Hell's Angels in which a fat man was stripped naked then murdered. There was a photograph of the victim in the book, King said, but he denied writing beneath the picture: 'Another good citizen snuffed out. Guess why?' King said he had written on the page opposite the photograph just the words: 'Another citizen snuffed out.'

Asked by Mr Wright if he considered himself 'a strictly truthful person', King replied: 'Not completely, no.' He said that on the night of Rosalyn's murder, he had taken eight or nine methedrine tablets and one of LSD. The drugs began to affect him at about 6 pm when a television set he was watching seemed to change its shape, appearing squashed. King remembered Rosalyn getting into the panel van but claimed to recall no more until he was at Mt Napier. Getting out of the van there, he walked about ten metres. He could hear music and bells ringing and saw animals in front of him, he said.

In his drugged state the trees looked grotesque, branches appearing as fingers, and he felt as though he was becoming a note in the music he could hear. He headed into the bush, he said, passing Lowery and Rosalyn before turning back: 'I could see Lowery hitting her. She was lying on the ground. He looked really grotesque with big hands, long legs and big feet,' he told the court. 'I sat down on what I thought was a chair, it was a tree, trying to work out in my mind what was going on. He was yelling but I don't know exactly what. I could not appreciate what was going on. I did not think anything was wrong. Lowery walked away and Rosalyn came over to me and put her arm around me and said: "Is Chris going to kill me?"'

King said he told her that he did not know. He walked away from Lowery and Rosalyn to vomit. When he stumbled back toward them, Lowery was wrapping the electrical flex around Rosalyn's neck. He said Lowery may have asked him to hold Rosalyn's legs. On the way back to the panel van, King said, he asked Lowery what had happened and Lowery replied: 'What, are you drunk or something?'

'I told him I was stoned and he laughed and said: "I killed Rosalyn. You helped me",' King said.

Melbourne University psychologist Professor Francis Cox told the court that he had examined both of the accused on 14 May while they were awaiting trial. While intelligence tests showed that Lowery 'functioned at the top end of the average population' other tests indicated that he had a psychopathic personality, said Professor Cox: 'He has an overall intense aggressiveness with poor control over these impulses and quite marked tendencies to behave impulsively.' In his 'impulsivity' Lowery appeared not to have the ability to take into consideration the rights and suffering of others that most people would consider normal. He had a self-centred type of personality, Professor Cox said, with only a small capacity to relate adequately to other people. Lowery showed a 'basic callousness' and experienced sadistic pleasure from observing the suffering of other people.

Professor Cox stated that in an interview with King he had found him to be of above-average intelligence. He went on to say that King displayed open contempt for Lowery: 'He was composed and showed rather little emotion except when he spoke about Lowery and then revealed openly his contempt,' he said. Professor Cox also said that King showed some impulsiveness and had a dependent type of personality. He had underlying feelings of depression and unhappiness. 'He has intense aggressive impulses over which his control was rather tenuous or rather weak. Sporadic acts of aggression are likely to be over and done with quickly and not be sustained,' he said, describing King as immature for his age, shallow and likely to be led or dominated. 'He could behave aggressively to comply with orders or demands of another person,' Professor Cox said. 'I would think there were two features consistent with this assertion — that he was taking drugs and, in particular, the underlying feeling of depression and passive dependent orientation.'

This evidence tended to support the contention that King had been led in the murder of Rosalyn by Lowery, but cross-examination by PD Cummins, assisting with Lowery's defence, made it all but irrelevant since Professor Cox admitted he had never tested King while King was under the influence of a similar cocktail of drugs and alcohol to the one he claimed to have taken on the night of the crime.

East Melbourne neurologist Dr John Ivan Bella gave evidence that he had examined King, using a test based on a reflection of the electrical activity of the brain. He found a mildly abnormal result frequently found in immature people or those with personality problems. He agreed with Professor Cox that King displayed a 'rather weak' personality. In answer to King's counsel Mr Ogden, Dr Bella said it was his opinion that people under the influence of LSD and methedrine might not be in complete control of their actions. 'A person would not be able to appreciate what was happening while under the influence of drugs,' he said. But Dr Bella told prosecutor Byrne that LSD by itself or mixed with methedrine could not cause amnesia, a view not entirely shared by Mental Health Authority psychiatrist Dr Henry Charles Bethune, who told the court that if King had taken the drugs he claimed to have taken, he would have been 'psychiatrically insane' on the night Rosalyn was killed.

Other psychiatrists gave evidence and expressed opinions on the effects of LSD and methedrine tending, as expert psychiatrists often do, to vary widely in their assessments of the short- and long-term effects of the drugs. It was, in any case, all hypothetical since the only evidence that King was drugged at the time of the murder came from the accused themselves.

Only Lowery and King know precisely what horrors they enacted upon Rosalyn, even though the autopsy report showed she had been extensively beaten and tortured. It is known that she was punched, kicked and stomped on while tied with the flex. Cigarette burns covered much of her body. After the fifteen-year-old had breathed her last, her battered, mutilated body was left among the rusting beer cans and litter of Mt Napier Reserve while her killers went off to play cards with Lowery's wife before going to see a horror movie.

If the accused were attempting to confuse the jury by shifting the blame on to each other, they failed. It took the jury just one hour and fifty-eight minutes to return the guilty verdict. The death sentence was then mandatory for murder Victoria, although it had not been carried out since the 1967 hanging of Pentridge prison escapee Ronald Ryan, convicted of murdering a prison officer. Ryan was, in fact, the last person in Australia to be legally executed by hanging. Trial judge Justice Smith donned the black cap and sentenced Lowery and King to the gallows. They were removed to Pentridge prison's notorious maximum security H Division where they were to languish in the condemned cells, uncertain of their future or the length of it, for two years until their sentences were commuted. During those two years, all appeal avenues were exhausted, including an appeal to the Privy Council in London, which reportedly took only forty-five minutes to decide them unworthy of clemency. Lord Morris, delivering the Privy Council's judgement, said the very nature of the killing showed it was sadistic and otherwise motiveless.

The Liberal Government of Victoria, led by Premier Rupert Hamer, later to become Sir Rupert, seemed in no rush to commute the death sentence. The media-dubbed 'thrill kill' of Rosalyn had polarised public opinion. Many believed the killers should die. Few — even the opponents of capital punishment, who probably outnumbered its proponents but were less vocal — could envisage successful rehabilitation of sadistic killers such as Lowery and King. When the State Executive Council finally decided, on 27 June 1973, that Lowery and King should be spared, each was sentenced to sixty years' gaol, with minimum terms of fifty years, which was believed to have been the longest specific term ever imposed by the Executive Council.

So Lowery and King, and their victim Rosalyn, faded from the headlines. The case did make brief news again when Rosalyn's mother, June, died from a brain tumour in December 1973, to be buried beside her daughter in the cemetery at Branxholme, about twenty kilometres south-west of Hamilton. It was at Branxholme that, at the age of nine, Rosalyn had been crowned Miss Junior Showgirl. Branxholme had been the family hometown until her parents divorced. Rosalyn and her mother then moved to Hamilton with Mrs Nolte's father, retired dairy farmer Roderick McCallum, to live in a rented house in Lonsdale Street.

Rosalyn's father, Ivan Nolte, was barely mentioned in the publicity surrounding the murder and subsequent trial, but he was 'discovered' by the media in 1992 when the case again made headlines. It was a newspaper reporter who told him Lowery and King were to be released after successfully seeking minimum gaol terms under the newly introduced Victorian Government Sentencing Act, 1991. The Act, in effect, meant that any prisoners serving life sentences could apply to the Supreme Court to have a fixed minimum term.

A public outcry against the release not only of Lowery and King but of several other notorious killers went unheard. Lowery and King were set free after the Adult Parole Board granted orders by Mr Justice Coldrey for their immediate release. Following normal procedure, their cases would be reviewed annually and they would remain under parole supervision until the expiration of their original sentences in 2021. Giving the reasons for his release orders, Justice Coldrey said both had been model prisoners who recognised their responsibility for their crime and had made considerable efforts to rehabilitate themselves while in gaol. Lowery had been involved in charity work, had studied religion and philosophy, taken up karate and become a Buddhist. He had also taken a course in the hospitality industry. Similarly, King had performed charity work, had gained a Bachelor of Arts degree and become involved in sports and drama. King had a fiancée waiting to marry him once he was out of gaol.

When told of their impending release Ivan Nolte, who had remarried after the divorce from Rosalyn's mother, said: 'I now have a twenty-three-year-old son. I don't sleep until he comes home . . . you'll think I'm a hard man but I'm not, but there hasn't been one second of the day where I wished those blokes spent every bit of their sixty-year sentences behind bars, unless of course it was their hanging. They'll get out one day young enough to start their own lives over. But who cares for my daughter? Her life was taken before she'd even experienced it. It's bad enough for one person to kill another but their crime was premeditated crime. They killed my girl for kicks. If they spent 100 years in gaol it still would not be enough of an apology for what they've done.'

Their release came soon after the then Police Minister, dour Scot Steve Crabb, had guaranteed Victorians there was no chance of Lowery and King being freed before the year 2000. His statement had been made in response to a media furore in 1988 following revelations that the killers had been allowed out of gaol on unsupervised weekend leave. In a letter to the Melbourne *Sun-News Pictorial* at that time, King wrote that he felt revulsion, pain and remorse over the brutal murder of Rosalyn. The *Sun* also spoke to his fiancée, described as an articulate, conservatively dressed, dark-haired woman, who told the newspaper that King was a 'loving, thoughtful, gentle person'. She was aged thirty-two and King was thirty-five at the time.

As some writers have suggested, in many cases of tandem murder one of the killing pair is the ringleader while the other carries out atrocious acts of violence in an attempt to please the dominant one. In the case of Lowery and King, while the evidence tends to support the contention that Lowery was the prime mover, it also suggests that King was a far from unwilling participant — which made him no less guilty in the eyes of the law. The available evidence makes it even more difficult to establish beyond doubt that Lowery was, in fact, the ringleader because the blame-shifting tactics used by the pair throughout their trial clouded the issue. It is further confused by psychiatric evidence given during the trial that King was the more intelligent of the pair and that both had weak and psychopathic personalities. What must be recognised here — and this is in no way intended as a criticism of the psychology or psychiatric professions — is that both are, to some extent, indefinite sciences. They deal with the darkest recesses of the human mind and the results of tests can be at least partially manipulated by intelligent subjects. When a number of psychologists or psychiatrists give conflicting evidence in a trial, it becomes difficult for the lay people on the jury to decide which expert is the most accurate in his or her assessment. One result of this is that juries sometimes tend to ignore the evidence they are uncertain of and make their decisions on the basis of the factual evidence before them.

In this case we find little evidence to suggest that the murder of Rosalyn Nolte was the kind of classic tandem killing described by Brian Masters, in which one strong and dominant personality controls and manipulates a weak and submissive partner. In Lowery and King we find two offenders who deliberately and callously took the life of a young girl simply to experience the thrill of sexually tormenting, and then killing, another human being.

It is difficult to understand what brought these two young men, both from hard-working and apparently caring families, to the point of committing such a brutal crime. There are some clues scattered within the evidence given at their trial. The fact that King is said to have regarded Lowery with contempt begs the question of his own courage. It appears King did not have the necessary guts to openly show his contempt for Lowery and refuse to be led by him. Indeed, it is likely that this contempt was a contributing factor in King's part in the torture and murder of Rosalyn. King may well have been exacting vengeance upon the helpless girl, subconsciously blaming her for his inability to reject Lowery's influence.

The involvement with motorcycle racing and the 'biker' image was probably another major factor in the behaviour of Lowery and King. Probably the only biker image available to Lowery and King at that time was the portrayal of American bikers in the Marlon Brando film *The Wild One*. While dramatic in its time, the bikers portrayed in that film don't compare with those of contemporary times. Today aspiring club members must earn their right to wear the colours, and they are subject, for better or worse, to the discipline of the organisation. This kind of biker culture was virtually unknown in country Australia at that time. Lowery and King would simply have had as their role model a Hollywood actor who, on screen, held ultimate power over all those around him. By linking their behaviour to the biker image, they almost certainly would have reinforced their feelings of God-like power over Rosalyn.

Even without the influence of drugs — and, remember, we have only the evidence of the pair themselves that drugs were involved — it is likely that while they were torturing and killing Rosalyn, they were totally divorced from reality, living out some kind of perverted, silver-screen fantasy and hardly aware that they would have to answer for their unspeakable crimes in the cold reality of their return to everyday life. It is also more likely than not that the drug claims were introduced only to attempt to make them appear less responsive for their crimes, in the same way that many people accused of some criminal offence claim to have had their judgement impaired by alcohol. It is strange, though, that this impairment rarely stretches to the point where they fail to try and cover up their crimes.

In the final analysis we can only speculate about Lowery and King's motives, but it appears the murder was the outcome of a prolonged period of exercising God-like power over Rosalyn; that in that time and place, the killers felt they had the power to do exactly what they wanted. They were not hampered by conscience and probably did not even consider that they would have to answer for their crime. In this, as we shall see in the following chapter, Lowery and King are remarkably similar to the sadistic perpetrators of the unspeakable horrors enacted upon an innocent young mother.

2

THE KILLING OF VIRGINIA MORSE

Crump and Baker

Any study of human behaviour is a journey into the unfathomable labyrinth of the mind. Psychiatrists and psychologists may come up with theories and place labels on certain mental illnesses and personality traits, but they are still as mystified as lay people about the intricacies of reasoning that allow some people to commit atrocious acts with no apparent remorse. Even a study of madness does not help a great deal since what most people consider to be illogical may well make perfect sense to a deranged mind; any attempt at understanding by a 'sane' person is doomed to fail unless that person has access to the same corrupt thought processes.

Kevin Garry Crump and Allan Baker are included in this work because, on the surface at least, they fit the classic personality profiles of tandem killers — a weaker person being coerced into committing horrendous acts in an effort to win the approval of a stronger person; in this case there is the added element of a homosexual relationship, which is not uncommon in male couples who commit tandem killings. Whether they were mad or just bad is a matter for the reader to ponder.

In May 1997 the New South Wales parliament drafted legislation specifically aimed at keeping that state's worst killers behind bars for life, among them Crump and Baker. The move followed a public outcry when it was revealed that Crump could have been paroled in 2003, despite his and Baker's papers being marked 'never to be released' when they were sentenced in 1974 for one of the most sadistic sex killings in Australia's criminal history. The case study that follows provides an outstanding example of a horrendous crime, the shock waves of which are still severely affecting people a quarter of a century after the event.

The sheer vastness and emptiness of the Australian bush provided the isolation necessary for Crump and Baker to carry out their crimes without interruption. Country townships clustered on the Newell Highway, which cuts through outback Queensland and New South Wales before finding its way into Victoria, probably see less excitement than most small towns. A traveller passing through some of these tiny settlements will see grain silos, railroad tracks, always a pub, possibly a church and, usually, a store cum petrol station. The reaction of most city-dwellers is to wonder why anyone lives there. Certainly locals would tell the traveller they would rather be in their hamlet than battling the rat race in Brisbane, Sydney or Melbourne. They, of course, know and appreciate the charm of country life at its best, feeling secure in the lack of action and consequent lack of threat. But how quickly those feelings of security dissipate when something sinister happens and, sadly, the history of Australian crime reveals that horrible crimes do occur in outback neighbourhoods.

That was the case in November 1973, when Virginia Gai Morse, grazier's wife and the mother of three young children, was abducted. Aged thirty-five, she was snatched from her home, held prisoner and systematically beaten, raped and tortured before being executed by her tormentors. Wednesday 7 November began, as most weekdays did for the Morse family at their property Barnaway Station, Collarenebri. Virginia's husband, Brian, spent some time working on a troublesome agricultural machine, a header, before breakfast. Following breakfast and last-minute preparations, the three children — aged eleven, nine and five — kissed their mother goodbye and went with their father in his car, to be dropped off at the school bus stop. Virginia finished tidying the kitchen before going into the built-in verandah that served as her sewing room, where she was close to completing a page boy's suit for her youngest to wear at her brother's wedding the coming weekend.

Everything was quiet and normal — except that none of the Morse family knew they had been under surveillance through binoculars since sunrise. The watchers were Allan Baker and his friend Kevin Crump. The pair had cemented their friendship as homosexual lovers in the prison where they'd met although Baker, at least, was far more interested in sexual relations with women, suggesting that the homosexual affair with Crump was a prison substitute for his preferred sexual practices. Both men were experienced criminals who had spent much of their lives behind bars for a range of property and minor assault convictions. Both also came from poor families and had histories of minor juvenile offending before graduating to more serious adult crime.

Baker was working as a farm hand, at Boggabilla in western New South Wales, when Crump, driving a car he had stolen at Aberdare, caught up with him on 2 November 1973. Work had been intermittent because of wet weather and prospects for the pair were bleak when they hit the road. The following day, Saturday 3 November, Ian James Lamb, forty-three and still living with his mother in their home at Gosford, on the New South Wales central coast, also hit the road in search of work. When his mother waved him goodbye at 6.30 am, little did she know it would be the last time she saw him alive. As Lamb was driving steadily deeper into New South Wales towards the Queensland border, Crump and Baker had already crossed it. They were in Goondiwindi that morning, the first Queensland town the Newell Highway reaches on its north-eastern journey and famous as the birthplace of Gunsynd, aka the Goondiwindi Grey, one of Australia's most cherished horse-racing champions.

But Crump and Baker were not there to admire the statue of Gunsynd. Having already decided that working for a living was as boring as it could be arduous, they bought a .308 rifle and ammunition with the intention of turning to robbery as a profession. Their next priority was to find a victim, a role that Lamb would play even though death or misfortune were probably far from his mind as his old car rolled on, not at great speed but carrying him inexorably towards a swift and pointless end.

As afternoon gave way to evening, Lamb pulled over to the side of the highway. He stretched out on the front seat of the car, leaving the windows partially open to allow some airflow, and settled down to sleep. Like so many Australians, he would not have given a thought to danger. He had little money, his car was old, his belongings meagre and, anyway, he was not in a big city, where drug-users, muggers and other assorted villains preyed on the weak. This was rural Australia, a place where there was safety in solitude and faith in the inherent good nature of country people; a place where many used to (and still do) leave their homes unlocked when they went out and, on warm nights, sleep with no more protection from the outside world than insect screens covering open windows and doors.

It was the night Lamb was to draw the short straw for no other reason than being in the wrong place at the wrong time. Crump and Baker spotted his parked car near the New South Wales township of Narrabri and decided to steal petrol from it. They pulled over and got out of their car. Baker took the rifle with him. Later, in his statement to police, he said: 'I loaded it and I walked over to the car and pointed the rifle through the window on the driver's side and I seen a man asleep on the front seat. Kevin looked in the back to see if he was by himself, and he was. I knocked on the door with my hands and said "Hey, you". The bloke sat up and I pulled the trigger and shot him.' When Crump made his statement to police, denying any responsibility for Lamb's death, he made a point of indicating the centre of his own throat to show where the bullet entered.

After the killing Baker went through Lamb's pockets, finding about $20. He also took some cigarettes and Lamb's wallet from the glove box. The pair then moved Lamb's body from the driver's seat, avoiding empty and bloodstained beer bottles on the floor, apparently having some difficulty untangling the dead man's feet from the brake and clutch pedals. Baker climbed in and drove the car, followed closely by Crump in the other car, to a deserted section of Bald Hills Road. There they punched a hole in the gas tank and drained it, loaded Lamb's few pathetic belongings into their car and drove off.

It appears it was after the murder of Lamb that Baker conceived the idea of robbing the Morse family. He had once worked for Brian Morse as a farm hand and lived with the family. He told Crump he knew there was a rifle at the homestead and there was also likely to be money. The pair cruised until the night of 6 November, when they camped within a few miles of Barnaway Station, striking out early the next morning to 'case' the Morse family home. It was from the cover of haystacks that they took turns watching the family through binoculars.

When Brian Morse drove his children to the school

bus stop and set off for his day's work, they moved in on the farmhouse. They realised another killing might be necessary and had already decided that Baker would probably be recognised by anyone on the property. In fact, Baker did not know that the youngest of the Morse children had started school and thought he might be with his mother. The decision to take Virginia Morse from her home and, as Crump said in his statement, 'get rid of her' seems to have been made before they entered the homestead even though the pair's stated motive for going to the property was to commit robbery. Baker was later to admit to police that they'd had every intention of killing Virginia and, if necessary, would have used her as a human shield against police bullets. It is difficult to know whether he was telling the truth or, perhaps, acting out some Hollywood fantasy and trying to impress the police with a tough-guy act.

At Baker's direction, Crump went to the back door of the farmhouse and knocked. When it was answered by Virginia, he asked if there was any casual work available; before she could reply, though, Baker's voice ordered her not to turn around. Of course she did, recognising Baker, who had the rifle muzzle pointed at her chest. Baker took Virginia into the bedroom at gunpoint and tied her up. When she asked what they wanted, Baker told her simply 'money'. They found about $30 in cash in the house and a .222 rifle. Taking the money and the firearm, they threw Virginia, still bound and gagged, into the rear seat of her family car and drove, ironically, to a police station. Unfortunately it was a ruined, disused station at Mogil Mogil, where they had hidden their car before going to the homestead.

Once there they transferred everything from the family car, including Virginia, into their car. They drained petrol from the Morse car to top up their own tank and decided to head over the border into Queensland. Driving mainly at night for the next 200 kilometres, Crump and Baker stopped occasionally to buy beer and petrol, and to take turns raping Virginia. Whenever the gag was removed from her mouth, Virginia showed that her major concern was for her children, rather than herself. Baker was to tell police she asked what was going to happen to her and pleaded: 'I love my children, please let me go home.'

By now the body of Ian Lamb had been discovered and Brian Morse had reported the disappearance of Virginia. Before long, police located the family car at the ruined police station. From exhaust burn marks and tyre tracks they began to build a picture of the car they were seeking, but it was already too late for Virginia. Close to the Queensland border, Crump and Baker pulled off the highway and found a clearing in the bush. Using towropes tied to saplings, they staked Virginia out on the ground, then each raped her again. By the time they eventually crossed the border and camped by the Weir River, Virginia was all out of tears.

Their statements about Virginia's last moments of life vary, with Crump and Baker each placing the major blame on the other — as we have seen, a common practice of tandem killers. Baker told police that Virginia was not tied to a tree at Weir River; instead, her hands were tied in front of her with handkerchiefs. He said he believed she was beyond crying because she had been crying most of the time she was gagged and blindfolded. Baker went on: 'I aimed at her with the .308 and Kevin had the .222 and it was going to be like a firing squad, and Kevin pulled the trigger and she fell to the ground before I could pull the trigger of my gun. If he hadn't shot her, I would because we both decided to kill her because we done those terrible things to her, and she would have been able to identify me because I used to work for her husband and I knew, if she reported me, we would be in a lot of trouble and she just had to be shot.'

Crump, on the other hand, claimed he was forced by Baker at gunpoint to shoot Virginia so that he, too, would be guilty of killing, because Baker had killed Lamb. He admitted to police that he had been prepared to kidnap Virginia and 'even sleep with her', apparently preferring the euphemism to the more honest word 'rape'. Claiming that Baker had bound, blindfolded and gagged Virginia prior to her death, Crump said Baker pointed his rifle at him and ordered him to pick up the .222 weapon.

Crump's statement continued: 'He said if I did not kill her he would kill me. I was forced to stand in front of Mrs Morse and Baker was saying, "Go on, go on", and waving his gun at me. I took aim at her but I just couldn't shoot her. I more or less dropped the gun to the ground and Baker started to wave his gun at me again. He said if I did not kill her he would shoot me . . . and I believed him. I took aim at her. I fired once. I shot her in the right side of the nose and killed her. I dropped the gun to the ground and walked to a raised portion of ground about 100 metres from where I was standing in front of Mrs Morse. I just stood there for a while and I drank a stubby of beer.'

Crump said that when he returned to the killing ground, Baker had stripped Virginia's body of clothing and was dragging it towards the river. Crump helped him to carry her to the river where she was dumped in the shallows. He and Baker concealed the body with tree branches. They decided to head for the crowded anonymity of Sydney but only managed to get as far as Maitland, near Newcastle, before their car was reported to police as one stolen from the neighbourhood on 30 October. In turn the car matched the description of one observed near the scene of Lamb's murder and was also compatible with vehicle clues left at the old Mogil Mogil police station, where the Morse family car had been abandoned.

Police were alerted to watch for the car and warned to approach its occupants with extreme caution. Around 11 am on 13 November, Senior Constable Jones was in a police car driven by Constable Millward. They joined Constable Neale who, in another police car, was close on the heels of Crump and Baker. Neale tried to force his way past the fugitive vehicle but was driven off the road by it. Millward and Jones managed to pull alongside the killers' car before Crump accelerated away. What followed was a running gun battle that could have been filmed for television. Baker was shooting at the police car through the rear window of the stolen car. Millward concentrated on driving while Jones drew his service pistol and returned fire.

Another police car joined the chase as one of Baker's rounds struck Millward in the forehead, fortunately failing to penetrate his skull. Baker laid down continuous fire as Constables Snedden and Hore took up the chase, but Crump overcooked his driving and the stolen car spun off the road. The chase and gunfight continued as Crump and Baker fled towards the Hunter River. As armed police encircled them, Crump and Baker's ammunition ran out and they surrendered.

At this stage Virginia's body had not been discovered, so although the pair admitted their involvement in Ian Lamb's death after the police found his possessions in Crump and Baker's car, they initially claimed to know nothing about Virginia's disappearance. The following day, questioned by Detective Sergeants Doyle and Campbell, Crump made his first admission relating to Virginia's death. When asked if he knew anything about the disappearance of a woman named Virginia Gai Morse, Crump replied: 'Yes. We took her away and shot her.'

The police were faced with a quandary. They charged Crump and Baker with the murder of Ian Lamb and the malicious wounding of Constable Millward with intent to prevent lawful apprehension, plus shooting at (a quaintly worded charge) with intent to prevent lawful apprehension, but they could not charge them with the murder of Virginia, which had taken place in Queensland. Loath to surrender their jurisdiction over the pair on the murder charge, they finally, and quite legally, charged them with conspiracy to murder Virginia Gai Morse, which could be substantiated by their kidnapping of her in New South Wales and their stated intention to kill her at that time.

Crump and Baker went on trial before Mr Justice Taylor, facing a litany of damning evidence. Neither took the witness stand but both made statements in their defence from the dock. In his statement, Baker denied intending to kill Ian Lamb, claiming Lamb had sat up suddenly in the car and made a noise, which led to Baker jumping backwards and the rifle firing accidentally. While he confessed to the killing of Virginia, he denied the conspiracy charge, claiming he and Crump made no decision to kill her until the day they did it — over the border in Queensland.

Crump denied intending any harm towards Ian Lamb other than tying him up and robbing him, and also said he did not think Baker was going to kill Lamb. He denied there was any agreement between himself and Baker to kill Virginia Morse, repeating his allegation that he had only shot her out of fear as Baker held a gun to him.

Media reports of the trial said Crump and Baker smirked at each other, treating evidence of Virginia's suffering at their hands as a joke. Her husband, Brian, spent much of the trial sitting with his head in his hands, a shattered man. He eventually left the court before Mr Justice Taylor finished passing sentence on the killers.

Crump and Baker were found guilty on all charges when the jury returned after deliberating for just one hour and forty-five minutes. In sentencing both to life imprisonment, Justice Taylor said they had outraged all accepted standards of the behaviour of men and the description of 'men' ill became them. 'You would be more aptly described as animals and obscene animals at that,' the judge said. 'I believe that you should spend the rest of your lives in gaol and there you should die. If ever there was a case where life imprisonment should mean what it says — imprisonment for the whole of your lives — this is it. If in the future some application is made that you be released on the grounds of clemency or of mercy, then I would venture to suggest to those who are entrusted with the task of determining whether you are entitled to it or not, that the measurement of your entitlement to either should be the clemency and mercy you extended to this woman when she begged for her life.'

Crump and Baker were removed to Long Bay's maximum security Katingal section where, despite Crump's attempts to blame Baker for everything, including his shooting of Virginia, they continued their homosexual relationship until the media intervened in the late 1970s. A television feature on Katingal showed the public that the pair was sexually and physically together just as they had been before the killings. The ensuing outcry led to them being separated, with Crump going to Maitland Prison and Baker being moved to Grafton.

Under the truth in sentencing legislation brought down by the New South Wales state government in 1989, prisoners sentenced to life could, after a wait of two years, apply for a definitive sentence. In 1993 Baker applied to have a minimum term set but was refused. Mr Justice Sully said his crimes were beyond understanding and as wicked as could be imagined. Crump waited until 1997 to try his luck, hoping it would be better, and it seemed for a while that it would. His application for his life term plus fifteen years to be reduced to a total of thirty years before becoming eligible to be considered for parole was granted. Crump, then forty-seven, had spent twenty-four years in prison.

Under a new victim's rights law which came into force only three days before Crump's application to the court, Brian Morse, now remarried, delivered an impact statement. Although his statement was made in confidence and kept private, for the first time Brian spoke to the media, saying it had been difficult for him to make the statement about things which he and his children had tried to put behind them. An advocate of capital punishment, Brian said there had been no end to the horror of Crump and Baker's actions for himself, his three children and his present wife. He argued that the full details of the atrocities Virginia suffered at Crump and Baker's hands should have been made public to give people the opportunity to look into the 'sub-human' minds of the killers.

Media regurgitation of the case and the possibility that Crump could be paroled within six years led to yet another public outcry and the rapid passage through state parliament of the Sentence Legislation Further Amendment Bill of 1997. Effectively the bill means that the most notorious killers in New South Wales will stay behind bars until they die. It forces the New South Wales Parole Board and the Serious Offenders Review Council to give the greatest weight to the instruction on a prisoner's papers 'never to be released'.

As always, the case leaves many questions in its wake. What was it that led Crump and Baker to cross the line from petty criminality to capital crime? Why did they find it necessary to kill Lamb rather than just rob him? Both had prison experience and it seems unlikely they could have been so stupid as to believe that killing Lamb would prevent a return to prison at some future time. And at what point was a conscious decision made, if ever, to allow the proposed robbery of the Morse home to escalate into the rape, torture and murder of a defenceless woman?

Despite claims during his application that Crump was a changed man, the New South Wales parliament was told that in 1994 he had been charged with the rape of an eighteen-year-old cellmate, a charge that was never proceeded with because the alleged victim committed suicide. It was also said that Crump had learned to read and write in gaol and had 'found God'. During that same period Brian Morse had given up the battle with the land and the family farm and moved to Sydney.

All the evidence indicated that Baker was the main instigator of the violence that occurred, but at the same time it is difficult to believe that Crump engaged in the killings simply because he was afraid of his partner. Indeed, as with other tandem murders we discuss in this book, there were ample opportunities for the so-called weaker partner to escape from his more dominant colleague. It is also unlikely that a case can be made to support Crump's claim that Baker forced him to take part in the murders at gunpoint. Their long and intimate association both before and after the killing of Lamb and Morse suggests that the bond between the two was hardly based on threat and fear. Why, if he was really afraid of Baker and really did not want to shoot Virginia Morse, did not Crump turn the .222 rifle on Baker? He held the means to defend himself and save Virginia's life in his hands, but still he shot her. Both men had a history of petty crime before they met in prison although there was nothing in their criminal history to suggest that either one of them was capable of the unmitigated violence that they committed.

Their homosexual relationship was an outgrowth of their prison experience rather than an indication of their permanent sexual orientation. Crump was probably more sexually committed to the relationship than Baker, but even then it is difficult to see that this commitment alone was compelling enough to force him to join Baker in carrying out two gruesome murders. What we will also never really know is whether, if they had not met in prison, either or both of them would have committed murder at some time in the future. What does look certain, though, is that both these tandem killers were equally responsible for the murders of Virginia Morse and Ian Lamb, and that Crump's explanation that he was forced to engage in the murders was a pathetic attempt to reduce his own culpability.

Tandem killers almost always place the blame on their partners in crime, holding the other responsible for coercing them into committing acts of extreme violence, as happened in Crump's blaming of Baker. While each person is unique and, therefore, each killer different, it is likely that this common pattern comes about following a sudden realisation that the crimes must be answered for. The manner in which Lamb was killed suggests that Baker had crossed the line between reality and fantasy by the time he squeezed the trigger. The simple act of possessing such a weapon as a .308 rifle may well have given him such feelings of power that, in that simple yet deadly action, Baker was taking revenge against anyone who had ever done wrong by him.

Admittedly this is simply speculation, but it is likely that Baker did not see himself as a callous killer when he shot the unsuspecting Lamb; rather, he saw himself as someone who had been wronged by the world who had decided to strike back. It didn't matter that Lamb was innocent and undeserving of any crime committed against him. It was what Lamb represented at that moment that cost him his life. Once Baker and Crump had murdered Lamb they faced limited choices: Baker could give himself up to the police; or Crump could refuse to accompany him further, although in this scenario he would risk being shot by Baker himself in order to prevent him going to the police; or they could both allow themselves to be swept along by the tide of a shared fantasy. As we know, they chose the last option. No longer were they at the mercy of the world. They were now in control and could do anything they liked. Their power grew out of the barrel of a gun. It made them omnipotent. It is almost certain that neither, at that time, gave any thought at all to the possibility of being captured. Most likely, neither could really conceive that they had committed a crime.

What followed would have continued to feed their egos and their fantasy long enough for them to destroy the Morse family through their unbelievably sadistic torture and murder of Virginia. Their existence within this fantasy probably lasted at least until the chase and shoot-out with police. Only when bullets began coming back at them would their fantasy have crumbled. This, then, was real life, and there was a very strong possibility either or both could be wounded or killed. Of course, this is not supposed to happen in a fantasy, so there would have been a rush of self-preservation which led to their surrender and Crump's subsequent blaming of Baker in an attempt to escape punishment.

The tandem murders we have examined so far have been examples of opportunistic killings. In country Victoria Rosalyn Nolte fell into place to fit the deadly fantasy dreamed up by Lowery and King; in outback New South Wales and Queensland, Virginia Morse fell prey to Crump and Baker because she and they were there. But in South Australia's supposedly staid capital city of Adelaide we find a pair of killers who set out to create their own opportunities. These are serial killers who, had it not been for a car accident and a funeral, might well have continued to terrorise that city.

3

THE TRURO MURDERS

Miller and Worrell

There could be no clearer example of hedonistic killers than James Miller and Christopher Worrell. Fulfilling every criteria defined by Dr Edward Green, Miller and Worrell took several lives for excitement or pleasure, engaged in acts of unspeakable violence, hunted their victims systematically, and obviously indulged in extreme sexual or erotic pleasure while they carried out their crimes. They may or may not have considered themselves God-like in their domination and elimination of their young female victims, but certainly their actions were those of people with no morality, compassion or concept of responsibility to society. The characters of these men who committed the Truro murders, as they became known, also strongly fit the dominant/submissive personality pattern typical of tandem killers; in fact, as we shall see, their relationship became the lamest of excuses by the surviving partner for his involvement in the murders.

Truro, like so many places in the British Isles, had its name brought to the colonies by people who wanted some connection with the home they had left behind.

One of those colonies was South Australia. Adelaide, the capital widely known as the 'city of churches', is generally thought by the residents of other states to be conservative, yet history shows that it has had more than its share of aberrant crime, including serial tandem murders. On the fringe of the famed wine-producing Barossa Valley, about eighty kilometres north-west of Adelaide, lies the Antipodean Truro. While the original Truro in Cornwall conjures up visions of wild natural beauty and Arthurian legends, Australia's Truro will be forever linked with shallow graves and the horror of serial killing — in particular, the disappearance of seven young women from the city of Adelaide within the space of two months in 1976–77.

These young women had simply been listed as missing persons until, on Anzac Day 1978, William Thomas decided to go mushrooming in desolate bushland off Swamp Road, Truro. On a visit to the site five days earlier, Thomas had found what he assumed to be the leg bone of a cow. He returned with his wife on 25 April, perhaps because of some niggling doubts, and examined the bone more closely. This time he saw that there was a shoe attached to the bone. When he turned the bone over and removed the shoe, he found human skin and neatly painted toenails. Thomas finally decided to call the police after he had located remnants of clothing, a bloodstain on the earth and more bones, including a skull.

The police investigation was, if not cursory, at best

routine. The remains were identified as those of missing Adelaide woman Veronica Knight, just eighteen at the time of her disappearance. Her passing was filed as murder but, with a cold trail, police had little chance of identifying any suspects. At the time they had no way of knowing that the bodies of other young women thought to be missing were scattered around the neighbourhood. It would be almost a year before four bushwalkers discovered the skeleton of sixteen-year-old Sylvia Pittman about one kilometre from where Veronica's remains had been found. Before that happened, though, the bodies of two other murder victims came to light, as a result of which Sergeant Bob Giles of the South Australian Police Major Crime Squad was assigned to seek a link between the cases. These two women were Maria Dickinson, twenty, whose skeletal remains were found at Murray Bridge, east of Adelaide on the main highway to Melbourne; and Lina Marciano, also twenty, whose body was found in a suburban garbage dump north of Adelaide. Maria, who had been missing for some eight months, had been shot in the head. Lina had been viciously beaten and stabbed many times.

Sergeant Giles, known to his workmates as 'Hugger', was unable to decipher similarities between the murders of Veronica, Maria and Lina, but he believed, as he told his boss, Detective Superintendent Ken Thorsen, that there was a strong connection between Veronica's disappearance and murder and the cases of six other young women who had been reported missing in the two months between

December 1976 and February 1977. Thorsen studied the reports and found that the similarities suggested by Giles were so convincing, he had to agree: the other girls were probably dead, like Veronica.

Giles was instructed to continue his investigation, which was extremely sensitive since the police could not risk the media being alerted. They feared that any publicity about the investigation would alert any serial killer who might be on the loose as well as causing panic in the community. They were also nervous of a backlash in the media against the police for taking so long to connect these cases and, perhaps, of being left open to accusations of costing more lives through their apparent tardiness. Giles also had to be discreet in talking to the families of the victims. He needed to learn all he could about the missing women and their last known movements without telling their families he suspected they had been murdered by a serial killer who was still at large, as this was a belief unsupported by any hard evidence.

When Police Commissioner Laurie Draper was briefed on the serial killer theory, he confirmed Thorsen's instructions to Giles — the Major Crime Squad was to continue the investigation in secrecy. Like police units the world over, the squad was short on personnel but Giles finally managed to gain the assistance of Sergeant Glen Lawrie and Senior Constable Peter Foster. While it was not yet certain all seven young women had become the victims of a single killer, Lawrie and Foster began working on that hypothesis and set about seeking a pattern. This meant comparing the similarities between the victims and the circumstances of their disappearances, including the locations and times of the last known sightings of the women, their ages, racial characteristics and appearance.

They also attempted a technique which was fairly new in Australia at that time: the psychological profiling of the suspected perpetrator. Profiling had been gaining credence among investigators after being pioneered and apparently used with considerable effect by the FBI's Behavioural Sciences Division, based at Quantico in Virginia. While such a psychological profile can never be more than a guide, it is a starting point in looking for someone with no known link to the victims. It is quite surprising how often these profiles turn out to be remarkably accurate when a killer is finally caught. The hardest crime of all to solve is the one where there is no known connection between the victim and the perpetrator, which is why psycho-sociopathic serial killers sometimes are able to continue their grisly trade for years before being caught. Psychological profiling does not totally overcome this problem, but it can help investigators get some useful idea of what kind of needle they are searching for in the haystack.

One question they considered was why the disappearances, for the purposes of this exercise presumed to be murders, had stopped at seven. The detectives decided the perpetrator was most likely to be a man who lived in Adelaide, probably in an inner suburb, who was a sex offender who'd spent time in gaol. They thought that he had probably been released prior to the first murder, and that the series had ceased because he was back in gaol. Lawrie and Foster concentrated their efforts on known sex offenders, working on the recognised principle that the behaviour of some sex offenders can escalate from comparatively mundane flashing, peeping and groping to more serious crime as the perpetrator feels the need to exercise more and more power over his victims.

While they were doing all this, the bushwalkers stumbled upon the body of Sylvia Pittman, which had the effect of throwing the investigation into top gear. Giles' original theory looked more likely than ever, and Thorsen called for help from the recently formed South Australian Police specialist section known as STAR force. At first his call for help was denied on the grounds that STAR force was about to carry out a major training exercise, but Thorsen went into bat with the commissioner and got everything he asked for. The discovery of Sylvia's body had also alerted the media, which, predictably, went into a frenzy. Truro became front-page news around the nation. The two apparent murder victims, Veronica Knight and Sylvia Pittman, were named, along with the other five missing women. The South Australian government offered a reward of $20 000 for information leading to the apprehension and conviction of the perpetrator or perpetrators, to which the *Adelaide Advertiser* daily newspaper added a further $10 000.

A massive police search of the Truro neighbourhood revealed two more skeletons in a field opposite the one where Veronica Knight's remains had been found. Forensic pathologists eventually identified them as Connie Iordanides, sixteen, and Vicki Howell, who at twenty-six was older than the other victims. Vicki, who was separated from her husband, had last been seen around 7 pm on 2 February, in Adelaide city. Connie had last been seen on 9 February, also around 7 pm, near her home in the suburb of Brooklyn Park.

The state government soon upped its reward to $30 000, making a total of $40 000 available to anyone willing to pass on worthwhile information. It worked. An informant came forward to tell police about incriminating statements made to her in February 1977 by a man called James Miller. The woman's identity was protected by police, who referred to her simply as 'Angela'. She had attended the funeral of Christopher Worrell, twenty-three, who had died in a car smash just eight days after the disappearance of the seventh missing woman, twenty-year-old Deborah Lamb. In her statement to police, Angela said after the funeral she had been talking to Miller in a friend's backyard. Miller, she said, was crying as he spoke of Worrell and talked about killing himself. Miller allegedly told her that he and Worrell used to pick up 'camp' men in order to shake them down for money under threat of revealing their homosexuality.

Angela said he told her that she did not really know

what Worrell was like and went on to say that he and Worrell had picked up women and killed them. 'I saw that he was serious about what he was saying so I questioned him further,' Angela's statement continued. 'He said he couldn't stop Chris [Worrell] from doing this, that he would just pick them up and rape them and strangle them. Jamie said he just drove the vehicle for Chris. I questioned him further about this and Jamie said that if I didn't believe him he would take me up to Blanchetown [near Truro] and show me the bodies of the girls they had killed. I got the impression from what he said that there were about six victims. Jamie said that one of them had been strangled with a guitar string. Jamie said he couldn't stop Chris from raping and killing these girls.'

Angela defended herself for not passing her information on to police earlier on the grounds that Worrell was dead. She said she was opposed to 'dobbing in' anyone, a truly Australian characteristic, and feared Miller would become a scapegoat for Worrell's crimes. No doubt the reward money would eventually salve her conscience on these points.

It is interesting to note that Miller allegedly said Worrell had become worse just before he died, and in fact the time lag between the killings had been getting shorter. Worrell, it appears, had been following the established behaviour of at least some serial killers. Despite popular belief to the contrary, he did not always kill by the same method, preferring to experiment with different ways of dealing out death. His confidence, it would seem, was building with each murder, increasing his boldness as well as his sadistic appetite. From the police viewpoint, Lawrie and Foster would have felt some satisfaction that Worrell was a near perfect fit for their profile. Shortly before the disappearance of the first of his victims, Veronica Knight, Worrell had been released from Adelaide's Yatala gaol, where he had been serving a term for attempted rape. If, indeed, it could be proved that he was the killer, then his death in the car smash would explain the fact that the crimes had ceased after the disappearance of Deborah Lamb.

Miller was quickly located by police despite living homelessly on Adelaide's streets, and on 23 May 1979 he was detained for questioning. Lawrie, who conducted the interview, had absolutely no evidence other than Angela's statement to connect Miller to the murders. He needed not only a confession but for Miller to reveal the burial sites of the remaining missing women. It was predictable that Miller would begin by denying any involvement. When confronted with Angela's statement, he suggested that she had concocted it in an effort to get the reward money, but Lawrie kept at him until Miller finally asked for a few minutes to think over his situation.

When Lawrie returned to the interview room, Miller said he had nothing to look forward to in life so he might as well tell the truth. He confessed to driving Worrell around and helping him pick up women. With almost disconcerting frankness, Miller said: 'We would take them for a drive and take them to Truro and Chris would rape them and kill them.' He offered to show Lawrie where they had disposed of the three victims as yet unaccounted for.

As the head of the Major Crime Squad, Thorsen still had responsibility for the investigation and since it was now 8 pm, he was legally obliged to either charge Miller, bail him or place him before a court. Miller had been advised of his rights but, so far, had not asked for legal representation. If he had done so at that point, he would almost certainly have been told by his lawyer to cease cooperating with the police to avoid further incriminating himself. Had Miller taken that course, the remaining bodies might never have been found and both Angela's statement and Miller's admissions to Lawrie could well have been discredited in any ensuing trial. A defence counsel would have seized upon the reward as Angela's motivation and no doubt would have accused police of 'verballing' Miller. Thorsen made the difficult decision to take up Miller's offer to show police the other graves and place him before the court at 10 am the next day.

A night search was organised and Miller, accompanied by Thorsen, Lawrie and Foster, was taken to Truro where other detectives, uniformed police, a forensic team and pathologist met them. There were also a couple of *Adelaide Advertiser* journalists to whom the story had been leaked. With the journalists remaining in the background, Miller unerringly led police to the skeleton of Julie Mykyta, sixteen, who had last been seen getting into a white Valiant station wagon in King William Street, Adelaide, at about 10.30 pm on 21 January 1977.

The entourage then moved on to Port Gawler, about fifty kilometres north of Adelaide. There Miller, after some initial difficulty remembering, finally pinpointed the makeshift grave of Deborah Lamb, whose naked body revealed that she has suffered the greatest violence of all the victims. The autopsy on her remains found sand and shell grit in her lungs, an indication that she had been buried while she was still alive. Deborah's ankles and wrists were tied with nylon cord, and her pantyhose was bound around her mouth and neck.

At first police were unable to locate a body at the third site Miller directed them to in Gillman, an isolated area on the fringe of Adelaide. It was not until later in the day that had dawned while they were recovering the remains of Deborah Lamb that a council grader called in by police located the skeleton of Tania Kenny, dressed only in a shirt. Tania was just fifteen when she went missing from an Adelaide street around noon on 12 January 1977.

Born in 1937 James Miller, an admitted homosexual who claimed he had never had sex with a woman, was one of six children from a poor family. With little education, he left home at an early age and made his living from odd labouring jobs or theft. His lifestyle inevitably led him into gaol, where he met and apparently became infatuated with slim, dark-haired Worrell. Already described by a trial judge as a 'depraved and disgusting human being', Worrell was serving six years for attempted rape and indecent assault. The pair entered a homosexual relationship and on their release from gaol chose to live together, sharing an apartment in the Adelaide suburb of Ovingham. Worrell, however, apparently said he preferred sex with women, so their relationship became more fraternal, although Miller was still totally enamoured of Worrell to the point where he would do anything for him.

As with many other tandem killers, the less dominant partner — Miller — claimed as part of his defence that he would have feared for his own life had he not carried out Worrell's instructions. To illustrate this point he told how Worrell had picked up Veronica Knight in Adelaide's main shopping area on the night of 23 December 1976. Just two days before Christmas, the stores were crammed with shoppers on last minute buying sprees. Miller claimed Worrell went for a walk, sending him on a drive around the block. After the second circuit, he saw Worrell waiting for him with Veronica, who had become separated from her companion in a busy shopping arcade. Worrell had chatted to her, learned of her predicament and offered to arrange a lift to get her back to her home at an inner city hostel run by the Salvation Army. By the time they climbed into Miller's car, Veronica, who in terms of mental development was slightly younger than her eighteen years of age, had been persuaded to go with them for a drive in the picturesque Adelaide hills.

After he had parked the car in a remote lane, Miller

admitted seeing Worrell force Veronica onto the back seat. Rather than come to the victim's aid, he walked off, giving Worrell around half an hour alone with her before returning. Miller told police that when he came back, Veronica was lying, fully dressed, on the floor in the rear of the car. Worrell, sitting in the front, told him he had raped and murdered her. Miller claimed he grabbed Worrell by his shirt, yelling at him that he was a fool. He said Worrell's response was to produce a knife which he jammed it against Miller's throat, threatening to kill him. Miller said he believed the threat and claimed Worrell repeated it later, when he was helping to conceal Veronica's body after they had driven it to Truro.

A similar story unfolded in relation to each of the murders. Miller helped to pick up the girls, drove where he was instructed, left his partner to indulge in his hideous pleasures, then returned to help dispose of the bodies. He did nothing to stop them — in fact, on at least one occasion, the murder of Tania Kenny, Miller allowed Worrell to use his own sister's home as the killing ground. Miller's sister was away when hitchhiker Tania was lured to the house and bound, gagged and strangled in the children's room. Her body was later transferred to a grave that had already been prepared. While Miller claimed that Worrell again threatened him with death if he refused to help dispose of the body, he also admitted helping in this instance because he feared involving his sister in the crime.

Each of the murders that Miller credited to Worrell

followed a similar modus operandi, with variation only in the level of pre-death violence. In the case of Julie Mykyta, the sixteen-year-old high school student had taken a job selling jewellery from a city stall to make a few dollars during her summer vacation. Running late at the end of the day on 21 January 1977, Julie had called her parents to tell them not to worry, she was on her way home. While she was waiting to catch her bus, Worrell used his disarming charm to persuade her to accept a lift from himself and Miller. Julie, it appears, fought back when Worrell attacked her in an isolated part of Port Wakefield Road, but her struggle was no more than a turn-on for Worrell — and Miller, returning from his customary walk, watched as Worrell knelt on her and strangled her with a piece of rope.

Miller's defence at his trial and his subsequent protestations of innocence ignore the fact that, on his own admission, he knew what Worrell was doing and knew beforehand what he was going to do. Even if he could not have prevented the first murder, he certainly could have gone to the police and saved the lives of Worrell's other victims. Under the law, his knowing complicity makes him as guilty of murder as Worrell, even if he did nothing to assist in the commission of the actual crimes.

Had Worrell lived, even more victims may have died and the perpetrators may never have become known. Miller's version of the truth does not exactly absolve him of guilt but it does leave an element of doubt, in that all the violence and killing were apparently committed by Worrell. The tale might well have been different had Worrell ever been able to tell it. The car accident which took Worrell's life on 19 February 1977 became the catalyst for Miller's arrest, trial and conviction. Miller had been a passenger in the car and received a broken shoulder. The other passenger, a woman named Deborah Skuse, was killed along with Worrell. In the conversation between Angela and Miller following Worrell's funeral, the informer revealed to Miller that Worrell had been suspected of having a blood clot on the brain. Apparently thinking this might have explained Worrell's penchant for brutal murder, Miller told Angela about the string of sex killings.

When Truro began to gain publicity as a killing ground some two years later and Angela decided to tell the police what she knew, she also claimed that Miller had said the victims were 'only rags' who deserved to be 'done in'. Naturally, Miller denied ever having said such things and continued to maintain he had had no part in the actual rapes and murders.

Miller was duly tried for the murders of all seven victims. He was convicted on six counts but found not guilty of the murder of victim number one, Veronica Knight. The jury apparently accepted his plea that he had no idea Worrell planned to kill her. The trial judge, Mr Justice Matheson, sentenced Miller to six life sentences, making no order in relation to a minimum term to be served. Miller has continued to seek a retrial, protesting his innocence even to the extent of going on a hunger strike for forty-three days in 1984. In April 2000, his application for leave to appeal the length of his non-parole period was refused. He is unlikely to be released until the year 2014.

In 1981 Anne-Marie Mykyta, the mother of Julie Mykyta, had her book *It's a Long Way to Truro* published. It is a heart-rending, poignant account of the effect upon a family of the brutal murder of a daughter and sister. The book gives a graphic insight into the thoughts and feelings of a grieving mother and the effects of the murder on her husband and son. It is, above all, starkly honest, as the following passage shows:

> *I was obsessed with images of decay; I could not eat; the smell of meat sickened me; it was like eating my daughter's body; and even vegetables seemed to be rotten in my mouth. I tried to block out the world with alcohol and Valium and romantic novels where everything always ends happily; but the world crept back, and I lay awake for long hours in the night; awake or asleep, I existed in a nightmare.*

Criminal investigations and trials can damage the victims and their loved ones as muchas — sometimes more than — the accused. The horror of the Truro murders remains, compounded by Miller's defence and the media implication that the seven women were in some way to blame for their own fate. Any reading of the evidence, or any assessment of the character of the victims, makes it clear that perhaps they were naive, but it reinforces without doubt the fact of their absolute innocence. These were attractive young women, some barely more than children yet to begin to experience life, who were plucked from Adelaide by two unfeeling, malevolent men, and used to satisfy an unspeakable lust.

The Truro case, however, has significance because it highlights yet again the weakness in the general proposition that one partner in tandem killings is so dominated and controlled by the other that he, or she, is forced into taking part in the murders. Miller was undoubtedly sexually infatuated with Worrell and feared losing whatever sexual pleasures he received, or gave, to his lover. Yet there is no real evidence that he was ever seriously physically threatened by Worrell or that his partner would have sought him out to harm him if he had left the murder scene before Worrell had killed his victim.

This was a relationship in which, at best, Miller, the passive follower of the pair, continued to associate himself with the more assertive Worrell because he feared losing the sexual and emotional bond that had formed between the two men. At worst, Miller's voyeuristic participation in the murders — even from, in some instances, a physical distance — ignited dark and pathological emotions of pleasure. By helping his lover rejoice in whatever forms of hedonistic satisfaction Worrell got from his passion for thrill killing, Miller was, even if indirectly, revelling in the spectre of the sexual violence that was the basis for the Truro murders.

Our next chapter takes us into the adolescent world of two youths who set out on what was to be an adventure but became a nightmare in which one died and the other was left emotionally scarred for life. It is a story that graphically illustrates the forces at play in the dominance–submission relationship between tandem killers and how the dominant partner revels in the power of exerting his will not only upon his weaker accomplice but on a helpless victim.

4

SOLDIERS OF DEATH

Reid and Luckman

It was early in the afternoon of 4 May 1982 that schoolboys Peter Aston and his friend Terry, both thirteen, were hitchhiking near the outer Brisbane suburb of Beenleigh. The boys were wagging school with the intention of making their way south. Peter's ambition was to hitch back to his old hometown in Melbourne in the hope of being reunited with his older brother Michael. Terry, just along for the ride, was planning to accompany Peter as far as the Gold Coast.

Peter was unhappy with his life in Queensland both at home and at school. A tall, lanky adolescent, he had suffered from myopia since the age of nine and had been forced to wear thick-lensed spectacles ever since. A gangly six-footer, he tended to be clumsy, which often made him the target of jokes and taunts by his peers. As a result he had never found it easy to make friends and the boys at his new school, Kingston State High, seemed little different to the ones he'd left behind in Melbourne. But this all changed during a class break when he was approached by a short boy whom he recognised as living near his new house in the economically depressed

REID AND LUCKMAN

Brisbane suburb of Marsden.

To Peter's surprise and subsequent relief the boy, Terry, was not looking for a fight. 'Hey, you with the specs, you live round near my place, don't you?' Terry had said, adding: 'Come on let's play footy.' From this point the two boys became close friends. By normal standards it was a less than constructive friendship. In the brief time that Peter and Terry were friends they regularly played truant from school and engaged in shoplifting sprees. Unfortunately, these habits would prove disastrous for the boys on that May afternoon as their path crossed that of two soldiers intent on sexually assaulting and murdering a child.

With little doubt the Reid–Luckman affair remains one of the most dramatic and disturbing examples of child murder in Australia's history. The incident involved two serving soldiers, both of whom came from disadvantaged and troubled backgrounds, and the interplay between homosexuality and violent sexual fantasies. Much of the media and public attention at the time was focused on the Chamberlain case, in which Michael and Lindy Chamberlain were accused of murdering their baby daughter Azaria at Ayers Rock (Uluru) in central Australia. Lindy's claims that a dingo had taken Azaria, whose body was never found, made great media copy and continued to do so for many years until the Chamberlains were eventually and belatedly exonerated. But the great dingo controversy was knocked off the front pages for a while by the murder of young

Peter Aston, a thrill killing that horrified all of Australia.

As Corporal Robin Reid, aged thirty-four, and Private Paul Wayne Luckman, aged seventeen, drove south on the Pacific Highway near Beenleigh, they saw Peter and Terry walking along the roadside. Reid recognised this as the opportunity he had been waiting for and pulled the yellow Daihatsu 4WD to the side of the road, some distance away from the pair. While Luckman waited inside the cabin, Reid opened the bonnet and leant over the engine, pretending to make repairs. Taking the soldier's bait, the two boys approached Reid and asked him if they could hitch a ride south; it was a request Reid was more than happy to accommodate. Without hesitation, Reid ushered Peter and Terry into the rear of the Daihatsu. As soon as they were in the vehicle, Luckman produced a rifle and pointed it at the pair while Reid threatened them with a knife. Ordered to keep quiet, the boys were quickly handcuffed and then driven sixty kilometres south, across the New South Wales border, to a beach near the sleepy coastal town of Kingscliff.

After they found a sufficiently isolated point along the beach, the soldiers stopped the 4WD and forced the two boys out of the vehicle. Almost immediately, Reid and Luckman focused their attention on the lanky figure of Peter. Terry was forced to watch as his closest friend was incessantly and systematically tortured by Reid and Luckman during a four-hour period.

Peter was repeatedly kicked and punched about the

body and head. He was then stripped of his clothing and hair was cut from his head and pubic region. Terry was forced to eat his friend's hair and then sexually assault him. Peter was also burned with lighted cigarettes, holes were punched in his earlobes with a leather punch, and an aerosol spray was ignited near his face. Peter's agony continued as he was bludgeoned around the head with a shovel and the wooden butt of a rifle, the latter breaking as a result of the violence with which Peter was struck. Luckman laughingly exclaimed to his companion, 'I'll have to buy you a new rifle.'

At one point Peter managed to break free from his tormentors, but the soldiers caught him again, subjecting him to further pain as they increased the force of their abuse. To prevent further escapes, they handcuffed Peter's ankles together and attached thumbcuffs to his big toes. While screaming for mercy, Peter was repeatedly stabbed about the neck and body. To stifle his cries, the boy's T-shirt was stuffed into his mouth. His throat was cut by Luckman, after which the two men rolled the dying boy into a shallow grave. Terry was forced to shovel sand onto his friend as the now unconscious boy took his last gasps of air.

In total, Peter's injuries included a depressed fracture of the skull, partial dislocation of the cervical spine, fifteen knife wounds, and severe bruising to the scrotum and penis. According to later reports by the Government Medical Officer, Dr John Follent, there were three causes of Peter Aston's death: haemorrhage, a depressed skull fracture and asphyxia. Post-mortem evidence suggested that the asphyxia, which ultimately ended Aston's life, occurred as a result of being buried alive in the sandy grave.

Late in the evening of 4 May, Reid and Luckman decided that it was time to return to Brisbane. Amazingly, in one of the strangest twists of this tragedy, the offenders took Terry with them, dropping him off near his home before continuing on to their quarters at the Enoggera Army Barracks in Brisbane. It was clear from subsequent statements made by Luckman and Reid that they thought they had frightened Terry so much that he would never recount to anyone what had happened on the beach at Kingscliff.

At approximately 1 am on 5 May, Luckman and Reid woke nineteen-year-old soldier Robert Ponzetti. Feigning stomach pains, Reid asked him to take him to the hospital. As the trio got into Ponzetti's Subaru sedan, the soldier was threatened at knife-point and ordered to cooperate. With Ponzetti as hostage, Luckman and Reid made their way toward the New South Wales border.

In the meantime, Terry had breathlessly awoken his mother and told her the incredible story of Peter's death. In horror, Terry's mother drove him to the Woodridge police station, where he recounted the day's events. Some time later, Queensland police officers accompanied Terry to the Tweed Heads police station. Together with New South Wales police, they began a search of Kingscliff beach. After bloodstains were found on tree leaves, the party soon located Peter's shallow grave.

Terry was questioned for several hours over the incident. He was able to provide police with a good description of the offenders and their vehicle. He also told them that the names he heard mentioned were Bob and Paul. Based on this information a search for the offenders began on both sides of the border .

Believing the police would by now have been alerted, Luckman and Reid concealed the Subaru behind some bushes at the side of the road and waited in hiding. In order to keep Ponzetti under control they bound and gagged him, forcing him to lie in the back seat of the vehicle. At daybreak they drove off to buy a newspaper to see whether their crime had been discovered yet. It had.

In another amazing twist, later that morning they released Ponzetti unharmed near Tenterfield in northern New South Wales. Threatening Ponzetti with death if he reported them, Luckman and Reid told him to say that his car had been stolen and to give police false descriptions of the two hitchhikers who had supposedly stolen it. Ignoring the threats, Ponzetti quickly made his way to Tenterfield police station, where he provided police with descriptions of the offenders and the vehicle they were driving.

By early afternoon police spotted Luckman and Reid driving south along the New England Highway. A pursuit took place and the pair were finally caught at a police roadblock near Glen Innes at about 1.30 pm. As he was being arrested, Reid turned to Luckman and said, 'Don't worry. We can write a book about this one day. Call it "The Hitchhiker".' At Glen Innes police station, Luckman and Reid were interviewed. Within hours Luckman had cracked under the pressure. 'We did it,' he said. 'But Reid did all the killing.' Reid's response was to blame Luckman — a scenario reminiscent of the Lowery and King murder we looked at in Chapter 1.

In a thirteen-page record of interview conducted by Detective Sergeant Peter Dunstan, Reid claimed that he was acting under the influence of some kind of external force. He said that while they were driving to the Gold Coast, he and his roommate picked up two boys who had stolen about twenty packets of cigarettes and were running away from home. He said that voices had told him to get rid of the bigger boy, Peter: 'They said they didn't like him, perhaps because he stole.' When questioned about the identity of 'they', Reid replied, 'I do not know the voices. They were deep, old-sounding.' This spiritual theme was later to reappear during the court proceedings in the form of an insanity claim.

Both Luckman and Reid were subsequently charged with the murder of Peter Aston. Reid was also charged with threatening to inflict bodily harm on Terry. The pair appeared before the Glen Innes court the next day and were remanded in custody to appear before the Tweed Heads Petty Sessions court in August. In order to develop a strong case against the pair, police began the unenviable task of collecting evidence, which included a search of the Enoggera Barracks and an in-depth investigation into the soldiers' backgrounds.

The police found a huge collection of knives, daggers and swords in Reid and Luckman's quarters. They also found pornographic photographs of male homosexuals in bondage poses. In a bag containing articles of Reid's clothing, police discovered a business card holder containing eighteen hair samples labelled pubic, stomach, arm and head, each of which was marked with a small identification card and a man's name. More disturbingly, however, investigators found essays describing encounters with young boys. One essay described a walk with a boy along a bush track. The writer recounted in his tale how he had produced a knife and held it to the boy's throat while holding him in a headlock and undressing him.

While searching Reid's car, police also found a number of books. They included the *Devil's Prayer Book*, *History of Witchcraft*, and *Satan's Bible*. As with other books of this nature, much of the content emphasised erotic and spiritual satisfaction derived from combining sexual encounters with violence.

One of the authors of this book, Paul Wilson, spent a considerable amount of time interviewing both Reid and Luckman, the investigating police and people who had known the two soldiers. It was from these interviews that the backgrounds of the two killers were established. Both men had suffered from disturbed and oppressive childhoods. Luckman came from a broken home and had poor relationships with his parents and his step-parents.

Initially he lived with his father and a step-mother, only meeting his real mother at the age of thirteen; she was living with an alcoholic who regularly bashed her.

Luckman had also begun a life as a homosexual prostitute, although he said that he had been forced into it by two men. In evidence presented during the trial, he stated that these men had approached him in the Melbourne suburb of St Kilda when he was thirteen. They asked him whether he had anywhere to stay that evening. When Luckman said that he didn't, the two men suggested their house as a possible option. According to Luckman's evidence, the two men sexually assaulted him over a four or five day period. He admitted that he initially found the experience traumatic, but after a while began to enjoy the men's company. 'I'd thought a lot about being with men,' he said. 'And I really knew what was going to happen when they asked me to stay with them.' Luckman admitted to the court that he had had homosexual interests before and after the St Kilda incident, and that at one time he used to dress up in women's clothes.

Luckman left school at sixteen supporting himself by working as a prostitute to supplement his unemployment benefits. At seventeen he joined the army in an attempt to find some direction in his life and escape from his unhappy family. Three months after joining the army, Luckman found himself transferred from Melbourne to the Enoggera Army Barracks.

As did Luckman, Reid came from a poor, working-class family. Born in the slums of England, he had come to Australia as a boy, later working at a variety of jobs, such as storeman, in Melbourne. Reid's relatives were described as 'a very good family — only working people and not well off'. Although it is unclear to what extent Reid suffered from trauma during his childhood, it is clear that he developed an obsession with knives and crossbows at an early age. Perhaps it was in part a desire to satisfy his obsession with weaponry that he joined the army in 1972.

When he arrived at the Enoggera Barracks, Luckman was directed to Reid, who was in charge of room assignments for the privates. Reid looked the young soldier up and down and was immediately attracted to him. Inviting Luckman into his room, Reid introduced himself and said, 'I can fix it that you stay here.' After noticing a collection of knives arranged in the shape of a flower on one wall and a collection of satanic books shelved on another, Luckman readily accepted Reid's offer. From this auspicious encounter, the pair became bonded through their sexual preferences, sexual fantasies and violent fixations.

Indicative of their obsession with violence, police gathered evidence of a conversation that took place between Luckman, Reid and another young soldier on 18 April. That evening the trio talked for several hours before going to a late-night film. The focus of the conversation eventually turned to torture. Reid apparently said, 'I would like to go out and kidnap two coons, torture and sacrifice them, preferably on a stone altar. I would not like to kill them. I would like to inflict pain before killing them.' Reid then described how he would bury them in shallow bushland graves where he believed they would remain undetected for up to twenty years. It was at this point that Reid pulled out a medical book and demonstrated how he would cut his victims. He then went on to say that cutting his victims and burning them with cigarettes would be the most effective means of torture without causing death. At this point, Reid allegedly produced two knives and used Luckman to demonstrate his methodology.

Of even more significance, however, was the fact that only two days before the Aston killing, Luckman and Reid had kidnapped another young hitchhiker. John Bruce was seized by the pair at gunpoint, blindfolded and handcuffed. He was beaten and threatened with death, eventually being returned to the road where they had picked him up. When asked during the trial why he had killed Peter and not John, Reid replied, 'I still had control of my reality and emotions in relation to John. We still had to abduct him and I thought we would terrorise him, okay, and we wouldn't take him to the police and my fantasies were being got at this stage. We set out to kill John Bruce but I couldn't and we let him go. But when we came to Peter it was getting stronger. Lack of sleep, other things, were building up within me ... the fantasies had got to me at this stage but ... there was no feeling, there was no satisfaction or feeling in me when I set out to kill Peter.'

On 4 August Luckman and Reid appeared before Magistrate Brian Hanrahan in Tweed Heads court, but the case was moved to Murwillumbah Court of Petty Sessions the next day because the conditions at Tweed Heads were noisy and cramped. The committal hearing was a media circus, with Luckman and Reid at the centre of a drama combining violence, sex and satanism.

During the committal proceedings, police produced a scribbled note that indicated that the soldiers had discussed the possibility of feigning insanity if caught. Detective Sergeant Jackson had caught a glimpse of Reid throwing it into a wastepaper bin at the Glen Innes police station. Part of the note read: 'After Luckman and myself had committed the offence we both mentioned to each other the possibility of using insanity as a means of getting off.' On 13 August, satisfied with the evidence presented before him, Hanrahan committed Luckman and Reid for trial in the New South Wales Supreme Court in Grafton. The trial was postponed, however, with the pair eventually appearing in the Supreme Court in Sydney before Mr Justice Adrian Roden and a jury of three women and nine men.

Part of the evidence collected by police consisted of a series of photographs depicting Aston's injuries. When the crown prosecutor, Mr David Shillington QC, went through these he decided that he could not present them to the jury because in doing so he might have risked psychological blocking by the jurors — that means that, faced with the horrific nature of the injuries, the jurors might subconsciously suppress the images, thus failing to recall the brutality of the offence. Justice Roden was relieved at the prosecution's decision, preferring that the jury hear about the brutality rather than see its consequences.

Although both Luckman and Reid disputed the degree of violence they were accused of inflicting on Aston, they didn't deny that they had inflicted grievous injuries. Where the two differed, however, was in the defences they used to try to reduce their individual responsibility for those injuries. Luckman claimed that Reid was responsible for most of those injuries, and where that wasn't the case, he said he was acting under duress from Reid and was not, therefore, a willing participant in the crime. In fact Luckman stated that he was forced to participate as a result of a direct threat. On the day of the offence, Reid had apparently asked Luckman to accompany him to the Gold Coast. When they got into the vehicle, Reid had pulled out a knife and said, 'We are going to kill someone tonight. If not, it will be you.'

Luckman's claims of duress were severely weakened in a number of ways. Firstly, Luckman appeared to make no attempt to escape from Reid. In this respect, Justice Roden suggested that Luckman could have escaped or at least stopped Reid on a number occasions both before and during the offence. For example, when the pair first encountered Peter and Terry walking down the road toward them, Reid had his head under the bonnet. At that point, Luckman had access to the rifle and could have turned it on him. Secondly, Luckman admitted to cutting Peter's throat and, among other things, hitting him over the head with the rifle. He also acknowledged that he made no attempt to help Peter in any way.

Finally, both offenders separately interfered with and tortured Peter Aston. The fact that they shovelled sand down his throat and burned his body with cigarettes indicated that they had probably rehearsed what they would do when they captured a victim. The kidnapping of John Bruce, several days before, pointed to the fact that the death of Peter Ashton was the culmination of the shared fantasies of Luckman and Reid.

In summing up Luckman's part, Justice Roden took into consideration his disturbed childhood, the rape and abuse he suffered at an early age, his homosexual and transexual tendencies, and the fact that he had received treatment in a psychiatric hospital several years before joining the army. Despite these factors, the judge was sure Luckman was responsible for the crime against Aston and that his traumatic upbringing could not be used to excuse his actions.

In contrast to Luckman, Reid chose to embark upon the road of 'not guilty by reason of insanity.' In New South Wales, the defence of insanity was open to Reid if he could prove that when he committed the offence he was labouring under such a defect of reason, caused by a disease of the mind, that he had no idea what he was doing. In support of his claim Reid argued that he was under stress as a result of his bisexuality and the possibility of the army discovering his sexual preferences and subsequently discharging him from the service. He also argued that he was suffering from work-related stress as a result of his responsibilities as a clerk in the Ordnance Corps. Readily admitting his obsession with witchcraft and the occult, Reid raised the spectre of 'the voices' and their influence over his behaviour.

Expert witnesses were called in to support Reid's insanity claims in the form of a psychologist, Mrs Kerans, and two psychiatrists, Oscar Schmalzbach and Bill Metcalf. Kerans' evidence failed to impress Justice Roden, suggesting only that Reid had a high IQ and was currently suffering from anxiety. Metcalf appeared briefly, stating that 'it was an appalling crime. I felt he would have to be pretty twisted to do what he did.' Schmalzbach's evidence was considerably more detailed and presented a greater challenge to the prosecution.

Schmalzbach considered Reid a dangerous psychopath, stating that 'in view of the existence of sadistic behaviour, squeezing the sex organ of the victim, the sexual fantasies, involvement in witchcraft with hallucinating experiences, allows us to think that a normal human being could not commit a homicide of this nature.' His circular argument suggested that Reid must have been mad because no normal individual could have committed such a horrific act. Schmalzbach was convinced that Reid would have been unable to reason with any degree of composure while committing the murder, and so was not responsible for his actions.

In an attempt to counter Schmalzbach's evidence, the prosecution brought in its own psychiatrist, William Barclay. Although Barclay's evidence was credible and contradicted that of Schmalzbach, it only complicated the insanity argument. As Justice Roden commented to the jury, if the law on mental illness is difficult enough for experts to understand, it is almost impossible for lay people.

On 26 November 1982 a verdict of guilty was handed down by the jury. They were able to cut through the confusing maze of legal evidence and conclude that both offenders knew exactly what they were doing. In their view Reid and Luckman were unquestionably responsible for their actions. Justice Roden sentenced both offenders to penal servitude for life, dismissing the argument that Luckman was acting under the influence of Reid. The judge's comment that this was 'one of the most brutal and callous crimes ever to come before the courts of this state' indicates the degree of contempt he felt for Reid and Luckman's actions.

Other than reports that Reid became a born-again Christian and a gaolhouse trader in consumer goods, little is known about his fate. It is likely that he has become lost in the bowels of the prison system, receiving that special form of treatment reserved for offenders against children, a crime that even the most hardened prisoners cannot countenance.

Luckman became a sought-after prison item, selling

his body to other prisoners for money and cigarettes. In 1989 he began hormone treatment while in Maitland gaol in an attempt to develop feminine characteristics in preparation for a full sex-change operation. The treatment began after a visiting psychiatrist assessed Luckman and reported that he was presenting himself in all respects as a woman. Shortly after, in 1990, Luckman changed his name to Nicole Louise Pearce by deed poll. Not surprisingly, there was government and public uproar over this type of medical service being provided to prisoners, particularly in view of the horrific nature of Luckman's crime. Even his mother has rejected Luckman, saying, 'I wouldn't let Paul back in the house to live now . . . I've got kids to worry about.'

As is often asked, who suffers the most — the victim or the survivors? While there is no definitive answer, we can only imagine the fear and suffering that Peter went through that day. Almost twenty years after the event, it is possible to observe at least some of the long-term impact the killing has had on Terry's life. After the murder he was taunted by schoolmates and community members about his involvement in the crime. At times he was confronted in the street, spat on and assaulted. Following the conclusion of the case, Terry became an inmate at a hospital, where he received psychiatric attention. Given his experiences, it is not surprising that Terry found himself in and out of prison for offences ranging from car theft to assault. In a pre-sentencing report for one such offence, it was noted that he demonstrated a great deal of anti-authoritarian behaviour, lack of anger management and suffered from alcohol and drug abuse. To date he still suffers from nightmares and flashbacks. As Terry's mother said, 'It has left an indelible scar on us all.'

Peter Aston's parents, George and Celia, attempted to divorce themselves from the loss of their son, but the wide media coverage made this virtually impossible. George had identified the mutilated remains of his son and was constantly haunted by the images, which in turn sparked a cycle of severe depression. Celia developed heart problems shortly after the murder and also spiralled into depression. They were awarded $20 000 under the Criminal Injuries Compensation Act for the mental shock and injury caused by Peter's death — a token gesture at best.

Unfortunately, the situation for both victims and survivors of violent crime remains grim. A guilty verdict and the handing down of a sentence, no matter how harsh, do little to relieve the pain and suffering endured by the victims of crime, and do little to compensate for the loss of a young life. This pain was revived again when Luckman sought parole in April 1998, but fortunately the New South Wales Parole Board denied his application.

Although Reid appeared to be the dominant personality in the relationship, Luckman clearly displayed intense enjoyment and satisfaction in the torture and murder of Peter Aston. Indeed, it is difficult to believe that he took part in the killing only as a result of being controlled or threatened by Reid. Although there were clearly homosexual undertones in the relationship between the two men, this was not the motivating force in the crime that they committed. Their sexual activity together was sporadic and lacked any emotional component. Reid consistently described himself as a bisexual who was more interested in women than men.

Instead, the relationship between these two killers was based more on their shared fantasies of violence and destruction than on mutual homosexual activity. When, after rehearsing of their fantasy, the two soldiers found an opportunity to act it out, they grasped the chance to discover whether the hedonistic pleasure of their obsessions matched reality. And although their joint pleasure in carrying out the fantasy may have seemed worthwhile in the short term, their feelings for and attachment to each other did not last beyond their capture. Acrimony and mutual blame marked their relationship from the moment they were taken into custody, and this hostility continued in subsequent years.

Tandem murderers are not always closely knit together in deep-seated psychological intimacy. Indeed, it would not have required much strength of will on either Reid's or Luckman's part to break their relationship and disengage from the violence that they ultimately committed. Few male tandem killers have the kind of unyielding bond and dominant–submissive relationship that so marked the infamous Leopold and Loeb case. In fact there did not seem to be much in the way of strong bonding even at the start of the Reid–Luckman friendship, and at times it was even difficult to be sure about which of them instigated the fantasies and violence they indulged in.

Late in 1999, Luckman was released on parole. The terms of his parole state that he must undergo regular psychiatric and psychological counselling, have no contact with either of the victims' families and he must not be in the company of a person under the age of eighteen unless there is a responsible adult present. He now lives as a woman in Melbourne.

At the time of writing, Reid's sentence was still to be redetermined under truth in sentencing laws.

MURDER IN TANDEM

5

KILLING FOR LOVE

The Birnies

Perth is an extremely modern and beautiful city which sits astride the magnificent Swan River. In the financially insane climate of the 1980s, Perth could boast more millionaire residents than any other Australian city, with the possible exception of Queenland's Gold Coast. But Perth, like all places, had its downside, including widespread political and police corruption, Aboriginal land rights disputes, a slowdown in the all-important mining industry and, last but not least, serial murder.

It was in February 1987 that David and Catherine Birnie were convicted of murdering four young women in what was undoubtedly one of the nation's worst examples of tandem killing. During a period of thirty-five days between October and November 1986, the couple engaged in a horrifying murder-for-sex spree that ended only when their fifth victim escaped from captivity and certain death. David and Catherine Birnie are yet another pair of tandem killers in which the dominance–submission theory plays a major role, yet the intricate psychological forces at work in their relationship seem to indicate that at times they reversed their roles.

The Birnies sexually assaulted then murdered Mary Neilson, twenty-two; Susannah Candy, fifteen; Noelene Patterson, thirty-one; and Denise Brown, twenty-one. They were also convicted of sexually assaulting a teenager, 'the one that got away'. She escaped from the couple's home and went to the police, providing them with vital information that ultimately led to the Birnies' arrest. The macabre story began to unfold when the teenager was reported missing. The fact that four young women had already been reported missing during the previous month alerted Perth detectives to suspect that a serial killer was at work.

The officer in charge of the earlier disappearances, Detective Sergeant Paul Ferguson, turned to Bill Neilson, former head of Perth CIB, for his expert opinion. Neilson's expertise was derived from a unique history with the Western Australian Police Force. During the 1960s he had been the officer in charge of the hunt for Eric Cooke, who was convicted of the murder of six people brutally slain over a four-year period. Neilson was eventually to see Cooke hanged in Fremantle prison in 1964. Neilson believed the current spate of disappearances bore a remarkable resemblance to those he had investigated in the Cooke case. He confirmed Ferguson's suspicion that police probably had multiple murders on their hands. Both he and Ferguson were puzzled, though, by the fact that at least two of the missing women had made telephone calls or written to friends and relatives after their disappearances.

Despite an exhaustive investigation, Ferguson's inquiries produced no leads. This all changed, though, when a half-naked woman staggered into a Fremantle shopping centre. After being taken to the local police station, this young woman recounted to Ferguson and his colleagues a chilling tale of captivity and sexual abuse. She told police that as she was walking along a street in an upmarket suburb of Perth, a man and a woman had abducted her and taken her to their house. They forcibly removed her clothes before chaining her wrists and ankles to a bed. The male repeatedly raped her while the female watched, alternately licking her partner's anus and testicles throughout the assaults.

During her period in captivity the teenager was resourceful, doodling coded messages on pieces of paper, including the Birnies' telephone number and a sketch of the house. Twenty-four hours later, while the couple was engaged in a drug deal in the lounge room, she escaped through a window and was able to tell police the address of her abductors. In subsequent interviews, the young woman told Ferguson and his colleague, Detective Sergeant Katich, that she had been forced to make telephone calls to her family telling them that she was all right. Police made the connection between this and the calls Susannah Candy and Denise Brown had made.

On 10 November, acting on the new information,

Christopher Lowery.

Charles King.

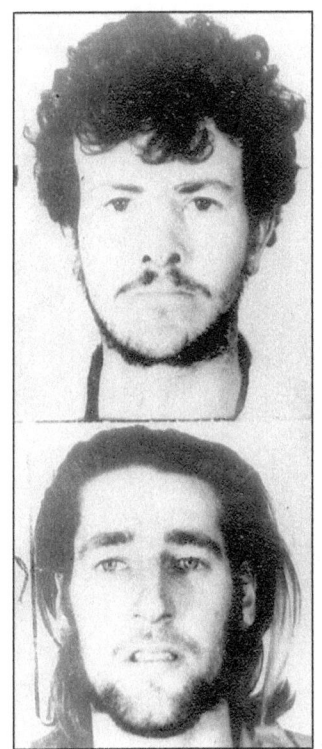

ABOVE: Virginia Gai Morse.

LEFT: Allan Baker (top) and Kevin Crump, gaoled for conspiring to murder Virginia Morse.

Christopher Worrell, whose death in a motor vehicle accident eventually led to the arrest of James Miller. Miller maintained that Worrell was the dominant partner in the Truro serial killings.

Veronica Knight, whose body was found by a man searching for mushrooms, was the first of the Truro victims to be discovered.

James Miller led police to the remains of Julie Mykyta, sixteen.

The remains of Tania Kenny, fifteen, being examined by forensic specialists after Miller located the burial site for police.

Truro killer James Miller leading the police to the graves of his victims.

Detective Peter Foster, of the South Australian Police Major Crimes Squad, carries bagged human remains from the Truro 'killing fields'.

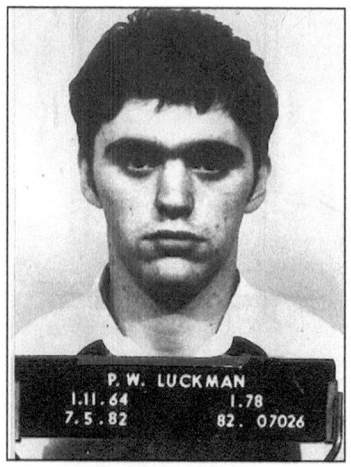
Paul Luckman.

David Birnie in police custody.

Catherine Birnie, flanked by policewomen.

Valmae Beck, being escorted by Homicide Squad detectives.

Beck's boyfriend, Barrie Watt, in police custody.

Cousins Vester (left) and Brendan Fernando, — the Walgett killers.

Cec Waters, the patriach of the famous boxing family, who died of a heart attack before facing the jury.

James Finch with his bride Cheryl Cole. The prison wedding was the beginning of a short-lived marriage.

Finch's partner in the Whiskey Au Go Go fire-bombing, John Andrew Stuart.

Dan Stuart, brother of John, who gave evidence against Stuart and Finch.

The blackened ruins of the Whiskey Au Go Go nightclub gives some indication of the intensity of the fire that took fifteen lives.

Harold Peckman being escorted by police from Russell Street police headquarters to the city watch-house.

Barry Robert Quinn — the catalyst for five murders in the sixty-nine days he was free after escaping from gaol.

CIB detectives staked out the Birnies' rented Willagee home. After a twenty-minute wait, Catherine Birnie arrived home and was immediately apprehended. She told police where to find David Birnie, who was arrested a short time later at a Perth spare parts centre where he worked as a labourer. David was taken into custody to be questioned at home with Catherine. Detectives made a thorough search of the Birnies' home, finding the escaped woman's cigarettes, lipstick and coded messages in the roof where the Birnies had hidden them. In light of the evidence against them, the Birnies acknowledged that the girl had stayed in the house, but they argued that she had been there of her own free will. David Birnie also admitted having sex with her but denied that it was rape, claiming she had given him consent.

The Birnies were taken to Fremantle CIB for more intense questioning. Ferguson and Katich were convinced the other disappearances were the work of the couple, but Catherine and David denied any involvement. Without a confession, there was little evidence to prove either the young woman's allegation or a connection with the disappearance of the other four women. Finally, David Birnie cracked under pressure, making the most remarkable admission. When Katich suggested, almost flippantly, 'It's getting dark ... best we take the shovel and dig them up,' David replied, 'Okay, there's four of them.' Soon after, hearing that David had confessed, Catherine Birnie confessed to her part in the crimes.

Later that evening, a police convoy escorting the

Birnies to the burial places of the victims wound its way to the state forest north of the city. David Birnie was particularly garrulous during the drive, so much so that he missed the turn-off into the forest where the first burial site was located. Birnie apologised to police. The convoy had to do a U-turn, backtracking for fifteen minutes before turning into the Gnangara pine plantation. The police vehicles moved along a side track for several hundred metres before David Birnie told the driver to stop, indicating where the first body was buried.

Katich later told a reporter he was looking for a mound of sand but could find nothing. 'I asked Birnie where the grave was,' Katich said, 'and Birnie replied: "You're standing on it".' Police were soon to uncover the decaying body of Denise Brown. After placing a guard at the first grave, the convoy moved off under the direction of Birnie to another forest site near the suburb of Armadale. The bodies of Mary Neilson and Susannah Candy were uncovered in shallow graves little more than a kilometre apart. Catherine Birnie then indicated that she would like to show police the position of the fourth and final body. She, like David, exhibited little remorse, appearing to enjoy the attention she was getting from the police. After identifying the location of Noelene Patterson's body, Catherine Birnie remarked to detectives that she hadn't liked her from the start.

To better understand some of the reasons why the Birnies committed these horrific crimes, it is necessary to consider their past. The way in which each was brought up as a child and their brooding and intense relationship are both vital clues to the murderous rampage they embarked upon. David was the eldest of six children raised in a very disturbed family where both parents were chronic alcoholics. The family lived on an eleven-acre property in Wattle Grove before they were separated. Family welfare authorities visisted the Birnies, regularly taking one or more of the children away from the parents to place them in foster homes or government institutions. At one stage David's parents were charged with neglecting their children. At the age of ten David was permanently removed from his home by the authorities.

David and Catherine had first met as toddlers, when their fathers worked together at the Royal Perth Hospital. Like David, Catherine had been raised in an environment that was devoid of many of the physical and emotional necessities of a normal childhood. Catherine was two when her mother died, and she was taken to South Africa to live with her father. After allegedly being sexually assaulted at the age of four, Catherine returned to the custody of her grandparents in Australia. Those who knew Catherine when she was growing up described her as lonely, always seeking attention, and generally unable to form any close relationships with either boys or girls. She had few toys and no playmates, but she was to find a friend in David Birnie when they met again as teenagers.

Catherine fell deeply in love with the insipid and

slightly weedy looking David. The pair became sexually active, with Catherine sneaking out at night to sleep with David. At that time David had been in and out of juvenile institutions for a series of minor property offences. Although he had little stability in his life, for a time he managed to hold down a job as a promising apprentice jockey. Unfortunately he was constantly the victim of practical jokes and taunts by other riders, and was eventually sacked after allegedly bashing and robbing the owner of a Belmont boarding house.

It was after the alleged bashing that David and Catherine embarked on a crime spree that landed both of them before the courts. On several occasions during 1969 the pair stood before the judiciary to answer multiple charges of breaking, entering and stealing. Catherine, then eighteen and pregnant with another man's child, was released on probation. David, also eighteen, was sentenced to three years' imprisonment. In June 1970 David broke out of the Karnet prison farm and found his way to Catherine once again. They committed another string of stealing or breaking and entering offences over a fourteen-day period. The pair was soon arrested and back before the courts. This time Catherine received a short gaol sentence. Several years were added to David's time.

While David was in gaol, Catherine worked for a family as a live-in domestic helper. She fell pregnant to the son of the family she lived with, and married him in 1972. He was a city council worker, and was deeply in love with Catherine, who was twenty-one by then. Although the marriage had hopeful and happy beginnings, it was to be marred by the tragic death of her seven-month-old son, Donny. The child had been accidentally crushed under the wheels of a car driven by a friend while his mother stood helplessly watching. The marriage continued, with Catherine giving birth to another five children, but it was not a happy one. After injuring his back, Catherine's husband found himself out work, and the family soon spiralled into a life of poverty. Living in a filthy and rundown housing commission home, and burdened with the care of her children as well as her father and uncle, Catherine sought refuge in the arms of David Birnie.

After an affair lasting more than two years, Catherine walked out on her family and took up residence with David. But her new household was just as disturbed as her previous one. For a start, David was living with an eighteen-year-old hairdresser with whom he was sexually active. On nights when the hairdresser was not home, David would have sex with Catherine. The bizarre love-triangle ended when the hairdresser moved out of the house. Catherine then had David all to herself. Although she never married him, Catherine changed her surname to Birnie by deed poll.

According to David's brother James — who was himself convicted of sexually assaulting his six-year-old niece — David was preoccupied with deviant sexual activities. David and Catherine would practise injecting

David's penis with an anaesthetic, would jointly share other women, and would copulate with each other in every conceivable way numerous times during any given day. His sexual appetite still unsatisfied, however, David began to conceive of more exciting ways to satisfy his needs. He also became bitter and angry towards women, with these emotions paralleling his desire to fulfil his deviant fantasies. He began talking to Catherine about abducting and raping young women. At first no mention was made of killing the women, but their joint fantasies of sexually assaulting innocent victims became more intense, until the couple could no longer resist acting them out.

The first unsuspecting victim to be lured into their trap was student Mary Neilson. At twenty-two Mary had been studying psychology at university for a number of years — in fact she was later to receive a Bachelor of Psychology, posthumously awarded by the University of Western Australia. Mary also worked part-time at an Attadale delicatessen, and she was last seen leaving there to attend a university lecture on 6 October 1986. Unfortunately she made a fatal detour via the Birnies' house on the way. Some time earlier, Mary had turned up at the spare parts yard where David worked, looking for some tyres. He suggested to her that she come by his Willagee home for a better deal. On that fateful October day Mary innocently took Birnie up on his offer. As soon as she entered the house, she was seized at knife-point and chained to a bed. David raped her as Catherine looked on. Apparently the fantasies that had been rehearsed by the pair in the past were played out, with Catherine asking David what it was like and how he was feeling.

Although there is little evidence to suggest that Catherine and David discussed killing the girl while the sexual assaults were taking place, both of them must have known that this was the inevitable outcome of their actions. And so it was. During the night they took Mary to the Gleneagles National Park where David continued to rape her. He placed a nylon cord around her neck and slowly tightened it until the young woman died. Mary was then buried in a shallow grave. Catherine later recounted how David had stabbed Mary's stomach, explaining that this action would allow the gases to escape, assisting with the decomposition of the body.

Catherine, when discussing the murders with her barrister, once told him she took part in the sexual assaults and killings to demonstrate her love for David. Certainly, during the rape and murder of Mary Neilson, Catherine kept asking David what it was that 'turned him on' and how he felt touching and assaulting each part of the young woman's body. It was David's pleasure that seemed most important in Catherine's mind, although her own voyeuristic satisfaction from watching the abuse of the young women was also evident.

After the murder of Mary Neilson, Catherine and David began searching for prey along the highways near Fremantle. They developed this practice into a fine art. Catherine usually drove while David looked for possible victims. Ultimately it was up to Catherine to decide whether a particular girl was suitable. During the two weeks after Mary's death, up to a dozen girls got into the Birnies' car and, having been given the thumbs-down by Catherine, made it safely out. Unfortunately, high-school student Susannah Candy, fifteen, was not so lucky.

Susannah was hitchhiking along the Stirling Highway in the suburb of Claremont when she heard a woman's voice calling her from a car. Catherine offered young Susannah a ride home, which she happily accepted. But when she climbed into the back seat of the car, David placed a kitchen knife to her throat, her hands were bound, and she was driven to the Birnies' home. Taken to the main bedroom, Susannah was sexually abused for hours. She was tied to the bed, gagged and repeatedly raped by David, with Catherine looking on. After the abuse, David tried to strangle the young girl with a nylon rope. She resisted strongly, so in the end he forced sleeping pills down her throat. When Susannah was asleep, David invited Catherine to demonstrate her love for him by killing the girl. Catherine had no hesitation in doing so. After a cord was placed around Susannah's neck, Catherine tightened it slowly until all signs of life had left the young body.

In his book *Never To Be Released,* Paul Kidd discusses Catherine's motives for following David's instructions. Apparently she explained to police: 'I wanted to see how strong I was within my inner self. I didn't feel a thing. I was prepared to follow him to the end of the earth and do anything to see that his desires were satisfied. She was a female. Females hurt and destroy males.'

The Birnies' third and oldest victim was thirty-one-year-old Noelene Patterson, a former steward for Ansett who had also worked on Alan Bond's private jet. At that time Bond was one of Australia's high-flying millionaires and the hero who had won the America's Cup for his nation. His empire was later to crumble and he would be gaoled. Noelene had been chief barmaid at the Nedlands Golf Club for about a year when one day her car ran out of fuel on the Canning Highway. Like Susannah, Noelene accepted a ride from the apparently friendly couple, only to find herself at knife-point once she got into their car. She was tied up and taken back to the Willagee house, where she was bound to the same bed as the other victims and, like them, continuously raped.

It appears from Catherine's account of this abduction that David was strongly attracted to his slim, elegant and quite striking victim. As a result, Catherine became extremely jealous and began to despise Noelene. Catherine's hatred intensified when David refused to kill Noelene, virtually keeping her as a sex slave for three days. Catherine felt personally tortured by David's infatuation. Placing a knife to her breast, she made it clear to him that he would have to choose between her and Noelene. Eventually David relented and, as he had done with Susannah Candy, he forced sleeping pills down Noelene's throat, strangling her while she slept. She was then buried, with considerable pleasure on Catherine's part, in a shallow grave near their other victims.

The Birnies' fourth victim was Denise Brown who, like Susannah Candy, was abducted from the Stirling Highway. A part-time computer operator and keen football supporter, Denise, twenty-one, was described by friends as a person who would do anything for anyone and trusted others too readily. She was last seen leaving the Coolbellup Hotel on 5 November by a girlfriend. The Birnies came across her while she was waiting for a bus to take her home. Accepting a ride with the couple, Denise found herself transported back to the Birnies' home where she was bound and raped, but not murdered. Instead she was taken to the Wanneroo pine plantation the next day where she was again raped before being killed.

This final murder was a particularly brutal affair. Catherine shone a torch for David while he thrust a knife into the neck of the young woman. He continued to rape her as he stabbed her. When Denise refused to die, Catherine suggested that a larger knife might be more appropriate. After the bigger knife had been used, Denise appeared to be dead and the couple began to bury her in a shallow grave. As they were covering her with sand, though, the Birnies noticed that she was still breathing. When Denise unexpectedly sat up in the grave, David grabbed an axe and viciously struck her head until she was clearly dead.

In later interviews with police, Catherine said that she felt guilty about the murder of Denise. She said she could see no end to the continual rape and murder of young women, and had a great fear that she 'would have to look at another killing like that of Denise Brown'. Apparently Catherine also had recurrent nightmares in which her victims would rise from the grave and try to pull her into it. Despite her claim of remorse and feelings of guilt, it is questionable just how much she really felt for the plight of the murdered women. There can be no doubt that she was actively involved in the killings of all four women. Although she stated that she took part only because of her infatuation with David Birnie, in fact she appeared to derive a great deal of personal satisfaction from the crimes, particularly the killing of Noelene Patterson.

On 12 November 1986 the Birnies appeared together before the Fremantle Magistrates Court charged with four counts of murder and one count of abduction and rape. With no plea entered and bail refused, the pair were remanded in custody until their appearance before the Perth Supreme Court on 10 February 1987. After pleading guilty before the Supreme Court to all offences, David was sentenced by Mr Justice Wallace to the maximum possible penalty of life imprisonment with strict security, and no parole for at least twenty years. In passing this sentence, Justice Wallace said, 'I am sorry that the legislation, as it is now, prevents me from adequately expressing what I believe to be the community's attitude to the punishment you should suffer. I am of the opinion that you are a danger to society and that you should not be released from prison ever.'

Awaiting a psychiatric report to determine her sanity,

Catherine was not required to plead on the day that David was sentenced. It was not until 3 March 1987, after receiving psychiatric clearance, that Catherine entered a plea of guilty to all charges. For the last time she and David clung to each other in the courtroom dock. Catherine was holding David's hand and rubbing his leg as the proceedings were finalised. Without hesitation, Justice Wallace gave her the same sentence that he had earlier given David: life imprisonment with strict security. In passing his judgement, Justice Wallace said to Catherine, 'In my opinion you should never be released to join David Birnie.' When Justice Wallace sentenced Catherine to a maximum gaol term, he made it very clear that he did not believe she had acted purely as a result of her infatuation with David Birnie. Nor was he convinced that she was as sorry about the murders as she had tried to claim to the police and the court.

Although her plea of guilty had spared the relatives of the victims the trauma of a trial, the judge maintained that he did not accept such pleas as necessarily reflecting the offender's remorse: 'This is because of my understanding of the active part you played in all the crimes, and I believe that the actions would have continued if you had not been discovered.' After listening to all the evidence, the judge went on to say that he was convinced that Catherine had willingly joined in the selection of the victims and had 'carried them off at knife-point and held them in captivity for the sole purpose of the sexual gratification of your partner in crime and then murdered them, lest you be identified, and then finally mutilated them'.

We cannot assume that Catherine experienced no pleasure or passion in the sexual activities that preceded each murder or, indeed, in assisting her lover to carry out the murders themselves. Her history with David suggests that the bond between them was strongly reinforced by the sexual activities they engaged in and by the increasing frequency and violence of these sexual escapades. Unlike the Reid–Luckman and Miller–Worrell relationships, sex was central to the bonding of the Birnies. While there is some doubt about whether Catherine would have continued to engage in these activities for the sole purpose of appeasing David, there can be no doubt about the strength of the attachment that remains between them to this day. Since their incarceration, they have exchanged thousands of letters. They have, however, been refused permission by the authorities to wed, make inter-prison visits, or to contact each other by telephone.

Catherine has talked about having found peace through Christianity while in prison, as well as developing an interest in saving other inmates from drugs. Several visitors to the prison have described her as a changed woman. She began a library course and assisted in the prison library at Bandyup, where she is serving her life sentence. Other prisoners have described Catherine as being particularly quiet and very much a loner.

Predictably, both Catherine and David have had a

difficult time in prison. Both live in fear of being attacked by other prisoners. David was bashed during his first month in prison and several threats to his life have been made by fellow prisoners. In 1987 he added another fourteen days to his sentence when he attempted to kill himself by swallowing forty sedative tablets. At the time of the suicide attempt, David was sharing a cell with his brother James, who was serving a sentence for breach of parole. Inmates have been quoted as saying that David gloated over his deeds, although Birnie himself has consistently denied these rumours and has argued that he is a changed man.

In 1993 David and another notorious criminal — child molester Bob Excell — obtained pornographic software to use on their personal computers in Casuarina Prison's special protection unit. The two were enrolled in a computer course and it is still unclear how they managed to obtain the erotic material. The publicity surrounding David Birnie's use of computer pornography provided fuel for those who considered that such material was responsible for the Birnies' crimes, although there is no clear evidence to support that theory. After the conviction of David and Catherine, the Censorship Office of the Western Australia Government wrote to the Assistant Commissioner of Crime requesting information concerning the alleged pornographic material found in the couple's Willagee house. The Assistant Commissioner replied to the request by saying 'searches of their home failed to locate any pornographic material in their possession'. He went on to say that although copies of *Playboy* were found, they were not considered pornographic and were legal in Western Australia.

In 1995, as a result of newspaper speculation that the Birnies were responsible for at least some of a number of unsolved high-profile Western Australian murders, David issued a public statement categorically denying any involvement in other murders. David stated that neither he nor Catherine 'had any involvement in any unsolved death or disappearance currently listed or under investigation by the WA Police Force'. In the same statement he denied that he had tortured any of the victims that they had admitted killing, saying that 'neither Catherine or myself would ever be party to inflicting further suffering on anyone'.

In light of evidence produced in court, the transparency of this lie throws doubt on the Birnies' denial of involvement in other murders. The very real possibility remains that one or both of the Birnies were involved in other, as yet unsolved murders. In fact David apparently mentioned other murders in telephone calls and letters to Perth law reform campaigner Brian Tennant.

Both of the Birnies hope to be released one day, something which is a very real possibility where Catherine is concerned. In the year 2006, Catherine will have served her minimum sentence, making her eligible for parole. In the case of David, however, any parole board would need to consider Justice Wallace's view that he was a danger to society and should never be released.

While we would not necessarily agree with the

general belief of the criminal justice community in Western Australia that Catherine's role in the murders was the result of her dependence on and love for David, that kind of view is not uncommon in tandem murders involving a man and a woman. For example, Brian Masters quotes approvingly from an unnamed psychologist who apparently examined Mrs Birnie; his conclusion was that he had never seen anyone so emotionally dependent on another person. Perhaps she was, but in our view Catherine Birnie does not entirely fit the submissive role. She acted with full awareness of what she was doing when she helped David to kill the four young women and, from the available evidence, it seems she took the dominant role in the murder of Noelene Patterson. She also appeared to gain considerable comfort from the sexual and murderous exploits of her lover in at least some of the cases. For her not only to approve but to watch and enjoy David's rape of their victims indicates that both were obsessed with sex. Readers may well be shocked that Catherine could be so dependent and apparently so much in love with David and yet not only accept but actually encourage and watch his sexual abuse of other women. This, however, is not such a rare phenomenon, as is illustrated by the tragic case in which a twelve-year-old Queensland girl was the victim.

6

MURDER FOR LUST

Watt and Beck

Less than twelve months after the conviction of David and Catherine Birnie in Western Australia, the horrendous events leading to their imprisonment were replayed in a remarkable string of parallels on Queensland's Sunshine Coast as an innocent twelve-year-old girl fell victim to the sexual obsessions of yet another murderous couple. In November 1987 the resort township of Noosa was to experience the horrific loss of one of its most beautiful daughters, schoolgirl Sian Kingi, in what remains Queensland's most disturbing example of murder for lust.

The killers, like Catherine and David Birnie, grew up under less than desirable circumstances. Valmae Faye Beck was raised in a poor and struggling family and had fallen in with the wrong crowd at a very young age. As a juvenile, she embarked on a career of petty crime that continued into adulthood. She was married twice and had six children. Her second husband had returned to Italy with their two children after the couple separated. Her partner, Barrie Watt, was perhaps even more disadvantaged. As an orphan he moved from Townsville to the Fiji Islands where he was raised by a pastor before moving to Melbourne. As a result of constant family arguments he left home when he was nineteen and fled to a life of crime in Perth.

Through mutual criminal acquaintances, Watt and Beck met in a small tavern in inner Perth in 1983. They were immediately attracted to each other and embarked upon an intimate and all-consuming relationship. After living together for several years, they married in December 1986. At forty-four and already a grandmother, Beck was her husband's senior by ten years, although he looked the older of the pair. Their life together consisted of a series of drinking binges in rundown old pubs and suburban parks, interspersed with court appearances for various criminal offences. Beck appeared to be infatuated with her husband and was prepared to bow to his whims without any apparent protest. Her acquiescence undoubtedly resulted in part from her view that age and frumpish looks made her relationship with Watt a fragile one.

In 1987 their criminal dispositions were to act as the catalyst for an interstate move. Watt was arrested by Perth detectives for armed robbery while, around the same time, Beck was arrested for false pretences. Surprisingly, both were released on bail. Realising that his impending conviction would undoubtedly land Watt in gaol, the pair decided to flee to a new life in Queensland. Driving via Melbourne, the couple traded in their small sedan for an HQ Holden station wagon. They arrived in the Sunshine State in October and rented a small A-frame house in the Brisbane Valley town of Lowood.

Despite being married for less than a year, the couple was already at loggerheads over Watt's continual penchant for younger women. In particular, he had an unhealthy obsession with schoolgirls. Given their age difference, it is little wonder that Beck felt threatened by his preferences. Totally co-dependent and fearful of losing his love, she was willing to do anything to keep him. Recognising his dominance over Beck, Watt suggested that she could save their marriage if she helped him carry out his fantasy of being the first and last person to have intercourse with a virgin. Watt held out the promise that once he'd had sex with someone for the first and only time, he would never look at another woman again. During November, Beck acquiesced to Watt's requests, and the couple started cruising the resort towns along the Sunshine Coast in search of a suitable victim. Given the selection criteria — a female virgin — the victim would need to be very young, a condition perfectly met by twelve-year-old Sian Kingi.

After school on Friday 27 November, Sian spent the late afternoon hours with her mother, Lynda Kingi, at the Noosa Fair Shopping Centre. Sian was blue-eyed, slender and very pretty, with long blonde hair and a healthy tanned complexion. She was particularly popular with her schoolmates and loved sport and other social activities. Shortly after 5 pm, Sian decided to ride her bike home while her mother walked. She was last seen riding her bike by friends playing at a local tennis court at approximately 5.30 pm.

As Sian rode through Pinaroo Park near the mouth of the Noosa River, she fell under the watchful eyes of Watt and Beck. By this stage Watt had consumed a large quantity of alcohol and had become extremely impatient and agitated. When he saw Sian, he said to Beck, 'There's a girl coming on a bike. Stop her. Talk to her.' Following Watt's instructions, Beck called out to Sian, asking whether she had seen a small poodle. As the pair conversed, Watt seized the unsuspecting girl from behind and dragged her screaming into the back of the white station wagon. The attack occurred out in the open within full view of the roadway. Unfortunately, nobody noticed.

With her mouth and hands taped, Sian was driven to the Tinbeerwah State Forest near Tewantin. She was taken from the car and subjected to a brutal sexual assault by Watt that lasted for approximately thirty minutes. After he had finished raping and sodomising her, he allowed Sian to put her blue-and-white striped school uniform back on. Then, using a belt from Beck's dress, Watt began strangling the schoolgirl. Still not satisfied, and with Sian gasping for her last breath, he stabbed her at least twelve times in the neck and chest region before cutting her throat. Dragging Sian's lifeless body by the ankles, Watt concealed her in nearby bushes. As if nothing had happened, Watt and Beck then drove to their home in Lowood. Beck had a shower and ran a bath for Watt before the pair retired for the evening in front of the television.

Concerned that Sian was late home, Mrs Kingi and her husband Barry began retracing their daughter's movements. They came across Sian's abandoned yellow bicycle in Pinaroo Park a short time later. Just after 8.30 pm the Kingis walked into Noosa police station to report Sian's disappearance. Although nobody in the park had actually seen the young girl, witnesses remembered seeing a white 1973–74 Holden station wagon in the area. All initial attempts to locate the girl or the suspect vehicle proved fruitless. As the days passed, the situation became more desperate. Detectives were called in from Brisbane and a full-scale search was undertaken using hundreds of local residents. A mannequin dressed as Sian was put on display outside the Noosa police station and at the local shopping centre in the hope of stimulating somebody's memory.

Six days after her abduction and murder, an orchard worker stumbled upon Sian's body as he walked through Tinbeerwah forest on his way to work. Noticing a pungent smell, he found the corpse under a tree just metres from the walking track. CIB detectives were called to the scene. Shortly afterwards, Detective Sergeant Neil Magnussen issued a warning to the local community: 'We have a maniac on the loose in the Noosa area. It is highly likely that he will kill again. No young woman should be allowed out of sight.' Using what little information they had, police intensified their search for the white Holden station wagon.

Interestingly, it was Beck and Watt's activities days prior to Sian's murder that provided police with a vital link to their identity. At about 5.30 pm on 11 November, the pair tried to abduct a shop assistant while she was reversing her car from the car park of the Target shopping centre at Booval, near Ipswich. Using a similar ploy to the one they had used with Sian Kingi, Beck approached the shop assistant and asked her for directions. Watt then walked to her car, turned the ignition off and held a kitchen knife to her ribs. Another Target employee happened onto the scene, causing Beck and Watt to flee. Later evidence in court suggested that Watt and Beck had already prepared a grave for the young woman.

Importantly, the shop assistant's statement to police contained at least two crucial pieces of information. First, the offenders' white station wagon had black-and-white numberplates and a registration number beginning with LLE, substantially reducing the possible pool of suspect vehicles. Secondly, the offenders were a man-and-woman team, a scenario that was not initially considered in the Kingi case. Police linked the Booval offenders to a couple seen at Pinaroo Park at the time of Sian's disappearance. The witness, who had seen the pair acting suspiciously, informed police that their white Holden station wagon had Victorian black-and-white numberplates.

As new information was integrated into the

investigation, police started to close in on Watt and Beck. Earlier, a uniformed police officer had noticed the station wagon in Lowood and made a mental note of the first part of the number plate, LLE. Piecing together the information, he contacted Noosa detectives and a search of the Lowood area was undertaken. Police eventually found their way to Watt and Beck's rented house only to find that the couple had left several days earlier. Eventually, police were able to pinpoint the couple's location to The Entrance, a popular seaside resort on the central coast of New South Wales. On 12 December New South Wales police, in conjunction with Queensland detectives, raided a motel in The Entrance and arrested them both. They appeared at Wyong court for extradition proceedings to face questioning over Sian's murder. They were also charged with the attempted abduction and assault of the shop assistant. The pair did not contest the application for extradition. After the proceedings they were transported back to Queensland on a commercial flight, under tight security and amidst death threats from members of the public.

Charged with the murder of Sian Kingi, Watt and Beck appeared before the Noosa Heads court. On the day of their appearance, a hostile crowd of nearly two hundred waited outside the courthouse. Among the those gathered were school friends of Sian, brought to the scene by their parents. Petitions were signed calling for harsher penalties for sex offenders, including the reinstatement of capital punishment. Placards with various angry messages were waved amongst the crowd: 'If they're guilty, I'd hang them'; 'Bring back capital punishment for crimes against our children'; and 'No air for these pair — hang em.' To complete the scene an executioner's noose was thrown over the flagpole outside the court. As Watt and Beck were escorted from the lock-up to the courtroom, rocks and bricks were thrown at them along with verbal condemnations.

During the proceedings, the court was told that Beck had signed a full confession relating to Sian's abduction, rape and murder. Given the nature of the case, the couple was remanded in custody to appear before the Noosa Magistrates Court in April 1988. At the April committal hearing, the court was told of secretly recorded conversations between Watt and Beck as they sat in adjacent cells in the Noosa lock-up. The tapes provide a remarkable and valuable insight into the relationship between the couple and their reactions to each other and their crimes. The first part of the tapes was recorded after Beck had spent the night being questioned by police. During the conversation, Watt asked Beck whether she had confessed. Avoiding the question, Beck said: 'We're going to gaol for life, Barrie.' Watt replied: 'You have turned into a really, really staunch wife. A real good wife, good loving wife, putting your husband straight into a murder rap. That is what you have done.' Beck then begged Watt to plead insanity.

In a later conversation, after he had been shown a copy

of Beck's police interview, Watt said to her: 'You hung me, good on you, top wife — if you hadn't betrayed me, we could have got away with it.' Beck replied: 'No jury in the land would have found us innocent. You know it and I know it.' But Watt retorted: 'No one seen us pick her up and throw her in the car, no one seen us kill her.' One of the recurring themes in the recordings was the couple's fear of prison life, given the fact they were child-killers — unquestionably the category of criminal most despised by other prison inmates and staff. When Beck asked: 'When we go to Boggo Road, will the female screws bash me?', Watt told her that she was likely to be bashed by everyone, not just the 'screws'. Watt then said that, as a result of Beck's confession to police, he could no longer protect her and yelled: 'Now we are going to be bashed for the rest of our lives. We are going to be bashed every day and murdered at any time.'

The pair went on to discuss a joint suicide and made an empty pact to carry through with it one week later, on their wedding anniversary.

'If you love me, you'll let me die together with you,' Beck pleaded. Later she said: 'Your heart is aching as much as mine, isn't it? Do you realise we've been married a year next week?'

'Next Saturday night, Mum, is our wedding anniversary,' Watt replied. 'Let it end then.'

At one point the recordings revealed that Beck felt some level of remorse, but this was clearly absent in Watt.

'Going out and raping someone is one thing,' Beck

rationalised, 'but to kill someone in cold blood and not have any compassion at all — that worried me. It's been worrying me for weeks and weeks and weeks.'

Watt's chilling reply was: 'I'd like to do it again.'

'Pardon?' said Beck.

'I'd like to do it again,' he reaffirmed.

'You see . . . and then you tell me you don't want to plead insanity,' Beck said.

Watt and Beck were tried separately. When she appeared on trial on 13 October 1988, Beck pleaded guilty to all charges except murder. During the proceedings, the court heard the secret tapes and listened in silence as Beck's statement was read. Throughout the nine-day trial, she showed no demonstrable emotion. Sitting in the dock with her eyes focused on the floor, she spoke only twice. On the two occasions when Beck was asked whether she would give evidence, she replied: 'No, no, Your Honour.' Beck's counsel, Mr Kerry Copley QC, said she had an abiding loyalty to her husband, who had made her do something against her principles and from which she received no pleasure. Mr Copley argued that Beck had actively sought to discourage Watt from murdering Sian.

It was clear from the evidence that Sian's murder was premeditated on the day she was killed. Crown prosecutor Mr Adrian Gundelach pointed out that Watt and Beck had made no attempt to disguise themselves or their car. Tape was not used to cover Sian's eyes but was placed over her mouth to prevent her from calling for help. Mr Gundelach said Watt and Beck knew that it did not matter what Sian saw because she would not live to tell anyone. 'She was meant to die and die quietly,' he told the jury.

The jury of nine men and three women deliberated for four hours before returning the verdict that Beck was guilty on all charges. In sentencing her to the maximum penalty of life imprisonment, the trial judge, Mr Justice Kelly, referred to Beck as a 'callous and depraved woman'. He commented: 'No decent person could not feel revulsion at what you did — and you, a woman with children of your own.'

It was in February 1990 that Watt was brought to trial before the Supreme Court of Queensland in Brisbane. He pleaded not guilty to all charges. His trial had been deferred while Beck went through the various avenues of appeal. Despite the evidence, Watt maintained throughout his trial that Beck had committed the offences. After an overnight deliberation, the jury found him guilty of all charges. The same judge, Mr Justice Kelly, presided over both trials. Watt, like Beck, was sentenced to life imprisonment. When sentencing Watt, Justice Kelly told him: 'The murder and rape was a particularly shocking and revolting crime, which shows you up as a thoroughly evil man devoid of any sense of morality. Life sentence is the only sentence for murder and, in your case, the sentence should mean just that. In my opinion, you should never be released.'

Given the nature of their crimes, both Beck and Watt were subjected to harassment by other prisoners during the early stages of their incarceration. Falling to the lowest level within the prison hierarchy with others, such as paedophiles, who had offended against children, they found themselves targets of physical assault and verbal abuse. In this respect the social conscience and disgust at such offences are shared by all groups within the community, including those serving prison sentences.

During 1998 Watt and Beck again came to public attention. Serving his sentence in Rockhampton prison, Watt made a formal request to the authorities to change his prison classification to minimum security. In conjunction with his request, Watt sent a letter to the Queensland daily newspaper *The Courier-Mail*, seeking public support for his application. Watt wrote in the letter: 'I stress that my past record makes it clear that I am not a repeat serious crime offender; I have no sex or violence offences on my record; I am not an escape risk; I maintain my innocence.' Later in the letter, he demonstrated his naivety in dealing with the media by saying: 'I ask that you and your office resist from using me as a political football when my case is next brought to your attention, in regard to my security rating. I have been made a scapegoat by the press and media and members of Parliament.'

Predictably, Watt's letter rallied little support for his cause and served mainly to remind the community of the bestial nature of his crimes. He attracted particular condemnation from the Homicide Victims Support Group, whose secretary, Ms Eleanor Harper, told *The Courier-Mail*:

'He wants a second chance. His victim was a decent little girl and he didn't give her any second chance.'

Beck's reappearance in the media was less dramatic but still managed to draw public condemnation. Her request to prison authorities to permit her to legally change her surname from Beck to Cramb was granted. Once this was done, her former name of Beck was added to the list of aliases on her criminal record. In response, the Victims of Crime Association president, Mr Ian Davies, asked *The Courier-Mail*: 'What gives these people the right to change their name? It would be one thing to do so when they leave [prison] but when they have been convicted of a horrendous crime, like she has been, they should serve the sentence under their name.'

The reclassification process worked more successfully for Beck and, at the time this book was written, she had been classified a medium security prisoner and sent to Stuart rison in Townsville. Her next step is the reduction to a low security rating, which will allow her unescorted weekend leave. In all probability, Beck will find herself on a work-to-release program before eventually being paroled.

The case of Watt and Beck might be used to reinforce the view that a stronger personality can influence and even manipulate a weaker individual who is infatuated with the dominant person. Watt, it has been suggested, was able to manipulate Beck to serve his own sickening ends, preying upon her insecurities and obsession for him. Indeed, Brisbane therapist Mary Fay explained

Beck's behaviour as the result of 'love addiction'.

In a comment to *The Courier-Mail* some time after the murder of Sian Kingi, Ms Fay said: 'They're prepared to do anything to keep a relationship. I've met Valmae Beck and I could understand how she would feel that without him [Watt] she would not survive. It's that unconscious behaviour: I may not like what he's doing and it may make me sick and I don't want to do it, but if it's the only way I can keep him, that's what I'll do.' Despite such causal explanations, it is impossible to overlook the fact that Beck was clearly a willing and active participant in the events leading to the murder of Sian. She was, after all, much older and probably more mature than Watt, and had had many opportunities to disengage from the rape and torture of the young girl — even opportunities to actively try to stop Watt from going through with it.

It should also be kept in mind that Beck watched for half an hour as Watt raped and cruelly abused their young victim. She also heard her boyfriend painfully and slowly strangling and stabbing Sian. 'She was making horrible gurgling noises,' Beck said. 'I know how the noises sound in my mind but I couldn't explain them to anyone else.' We have only Beck's statement at her trial as evidence that she took their dog to the other side of the car during the period in which Watt strangled Sian. Even if we accept her statement, she also admitted that she had 'seen [Sian's] legs moving' and that she had done absolutely nothing to try and stop this horrible crime from being perpetrated within a few metres of where she was standing.

It defies normal understanding that anyone in love, no matter how desperately, would allow themselves to be coerced into committing acts of unspeakable depravity for the sake of holding on to a relationship. Without some level of self-gratification, the supposedly insecure, weaker partner would certainly refuse to become involved in these acts and would most likely take some steps to stop them from happening. Love is an emotion that can hardly be separated from compassion; in most cases, a person truly in love is also a person with feelings of warmth and compassion for the rest of the world. It is ironic that love — that most tender of all human emotions — plays such an integral part in so many tragedies. It was love that, in our next chapter, would take an intelligent and attractive young nurse to country New South Wales, where she was to become an innocent victim.

7

OPPORTUNITY KILLING

The Fernando Cousins

Walgett, in north-western New South Wales, is a small country town, not much different than other country towns in the state. In December 1994, like much of rural Australia, Walgett was in the grip of a crippling drought. The thoughts of the locals rarely strayed from worrying about the lack of rain and how they were to survive until the rains came. No one would have suspected that Walgett was about to become the scene of a sex murder of unbelievable savagery. The victim, twenty-one-year-old nurse Sandra Hoare, had moved from her Sydney home to Walgett to live with her fiancé, local police constable David Taylor. They planned to marry early in 1995. Sandra's death was to lead to extensive upgrading of security measures for nurses working night shifts in the state's hospitals — a measure that came much too late for one nurse.

Sandra was a quiet, pretty young woman with a cascade of dark curling hair. Her selection as a victim of rape, torture and murder came about for no other reason than that she was in the wrong place at the wrong time, so often the criteria on which victims are chosen.

On the night of 8 December, she was working the night shift alone in Walgett Hospital's Peg Cross geriatric ward — one of the legion of nurses across Australia who take enormous responsibility working the night shift at remote hospitals with little or no back-up.

In this case, the tandem killers were cousins Brendan Fernando and Vester Allen Fernando. Brendan was twenty-five and Vester twenty-seven when they faced trial for Sandra's murder. It is unusual for people who kill in tandem to be blood relatives. Although the majority of partners in a murderous couple have known each other for some time, it is rare for them to have kin relationship. Where the killers are a male and female couple, their relationship is usually that of boyfriend–girlfriend or, as in some of the cases in this book, husband and wife.

Once again the dominance–submission theory is relevant here, although in this case the relationship was not based on the sexual or mutual dependency of the partners. It appears that their blood relationship allowed Vester, the senior partner by two years and intellectually superior, to dominate Brendan, who was quite used to following his cousin's lead. In fact, although both Fernandos were convicted of Sandra's murder and acted in concert up to the point of the killing, it was claimed at the trial that Brendan was actually walking away from the scene when Vester delivered the mortal blow. Nonetheless, Brendan could have walked away at any time and sought help for Sandra before the murder took place; he chose not to do so.

It is important in this case to acknowledge that the Fernandos are Aboriginal, and that their racial origin may have played some part in the murders. One of the authors, Paul Wilson, has argued (in another book *Black Death White Hands*) that the disintegration of traditional Aboriginal society brought about by white colonisation has led to the crumbling of personal and community restraints, resulting in high rates of suicide and violence towards others. In fact there is considerable evidence to show that levels of violence increase in indigenous communities that have been torn apart by forced resettlement and the erosion of language, customs and traditional forms of authority and control.

The racial distinction is significant in this case because there can be no doubt that the Fernandos came from a background in which unemployment, drugs and alcohol were major influences on their lives. Of course, these factors do not absolve the two offenders for their actions, but they go a long way towards explaining the hopelessness of their lives and the circumstances that led to the senseless murder of Sandra. Without doubt, neglect of Australia's Aboriginal population is a national disgrace, and one which most non-Aboriginal people are happy to ignore. The Fernandos did not kill Sandra because they are Aborigines; it was a crime that grew out of the utter futility of their existence, and the fact that they cared so little for themselves that they were certainly beyond caring what they did to anyone else.

Brendan was one of eight children. His father, a cotton worker who was forced to travel far in search of work to support his family, was working away from home when his heart gave up on him. Brendan was fifteen when his father died. His father's brother, Keith, father of Vester, also had eight children to feed and was a hard-working shearer until his health failed, leaving him and his family to survive on an invalid pension. The year after his father died, Brendan was 'asked to leave' Walgett High School. Vester had already given up schooling, although reportedly he could barely read. The two boys found companionship and trouble together. Both began to build criminal records from a young age.

While in Sydney's Long Bay gaol awaiting trial, Brendan was put through a series of tests by the head of behavioural sciences at the University of Sydney, Professor Susan Hayes. Professor Hayes concluded that Brendan was probably brain damaged after years of alcohol consumption, gasoline sniffing and heroin using — in fact there was evidence to show that Brendan had begun smoking marijuana at the age of ten. Professor Hayes determined that Brendan had an IQ of 59, the ability of a seven-year-old to form relationships and the coping skills of a six-year-old. During the trial the court was told that by the time he was charged, Brendan already had five children by three different mothers; and he had first become a father at the age of sixteen. The court was also told that Vester, too, was seriously addicted to alcohol, frequently used the drug Serepax, and had been under the influence of one or both drugs each time he had committed an offence.

Thursday 8 December was sultry as the humidity level rose creating the need for liquid sustenance among the residents, a number of whom chose whatever alcoholic beverages they could afford because it was also payday for those receiving social security benefits. Even small towns have their poor neighbourhoods, and it was on the west side of Walgett that Brendan lived with his sister Kerry and her de facto husband, Trimby Morris. Since no one had a job to go to, the three went over to the home of Iris Fernando, mother of Brendan and Kerry. Around 11 am they began a serious drinking session. During that day, with the help of some mates, Brendan and Trimby went through four dozen stubbies of beer. Brendan was well and truly drunk by the time he met Vester, who had arrived back in Walgett after quitting a drying-out hostel near Brewarrina, some seventy kilometres distant.

The pair met near the Imperial Hotel just after closing time to finish off beer bought from the bottle shop. They separated for a while to wander the streets of Walgett, then met again before dropping into Brendan's home to pick up some marijuana joints. When they left, saying they were going in search of more drinks, Vester had a bag of marijuana with him. Around 11.30 pm they were involved in a street incident when Vester grabbed nineteen-year-old Robert 'Fatboy' Walford and threatened him with a machete, apparently over some wrong Walford had done to Vester's father. Walford escaped without injury but the threatened attack on him was later to help lead the police to Vester during their investigation of Sandra's murder.

Vester and Brendan continued their wanderings and since quite a few people, mostly Aborigines and very young, were hanging around the streets of Walgett, the cousins were seen by plenty of witnesses. They shared a joint outside a tyre service workshop with Michael Jackson, nineteen. Jackson said they talked to him about stealing a car but he wasn't interested. During their conversation, a witness overheard Vester's plan to go to Walgett Hospital and steal a car.

When Vester and Brendan broke into a blue Sigma station wagon in the hospital car park, they were spotted by Sandra through a window. Brendan claimed Vester sent him inside to prevent her from raising the alarm. Vester then went to the ward, entering through another door, and grabbed Sandra after bashing an aging male patient who tried to help her. The next hour was undoubtedly the longest and most terrifying of Sandra's young life. Threatened by Vester with his machete, she was taken to an isolated sports oval where she was bashed, stripped and sexually assaulted. During this assault, Brendan held Sandra by the legs. She was apparently permitted to put her slacks back on before being forced to walk to a field about half a kilometre away. There Vester killed her, the blow he delivered with his machete almost severing her head. Brendan, who claimed to have been walking away at the time, said he heard her scream once.

After Sandra's body was discovered, the police quickly gleaned information from Walgett locals. The time was approaching 1 am on Saturday 10 December when they awakened Brendan at his sister's house and began questioning. Brendan allegedly made statements linking him and Vester to the murder, but he claimed that he did not have sex with Sandra and was walking away when Vester killed her. Vester left Walgett early on the Saturday morning and headed for Dubbo, where he was eventually detained at his sister's house. He refused to provide the police with hair and blood samples, refused to have his interview recorded electronically and claimed he had been asleep in Walgett at the time Sandra was murdered.

At the trial of the cousins, presided over by Mr Justice Alan Abadee, police procedure in dealing with Brendan was questioned. It was alleged that Brendan had not been cautioned by police before being interviewed at home, and that he was unable to understand the caution put to him at the police station when he was taken there for further questioning. In fact Professor Hayes said she had severe doubts about whether Brendan would have been able to comprehend what was happening during his trial.

In June 1997, the jury took little more than two hours to find the cousins guilty of murder. They were sentenced to life in gaol which, under the New South Wales 1989 truth-in-sentencing legislation, meant neither was likely to see the outside world again.

Before they were sentenced counsel for Vester, Mr Gabriel Wendler, had argued that for a life sentence to be imposed the case must be found to be in the 'worst category': 'This is a serious piece of offending but it's not in the worst category known to criminal law,' Wendler claimed. Justice Abadee disagreed strongly, saying: 'To almost behead someone would put itself into the worst category . . . especially if it is a defenceless woman.'

Justice Abadee went on to say that during her ordeal Sandra was subjected to degradation and humiliation as well as mental torture, terror and great fear. She had received horrendous, savage injuries inflicted with extraordinary force, and the punishment should be seen to fit the crime and to reflect the community's interest in retribution. 'May I add this message by way of some plain speaking to those persons who might be tempted,' Justice Abadee said. 'Reflect for a moment about your age and where you may spend the rest of your life.' Justice Abadee said life expectancy tables showed the cousins could expect to spend forty-nine or fifty years in gaol.

Keith Fernando, speaking in court for his son Vester, said: 'I think that drinking is the main problem for all the Aboriginal children in Walgett. All they've got to do is stand around the street and drink.' Outside the court after the trial, Sandra's mother Pauline described Justice Abadee as very fair, saying his judgement was common sense. She said the sentences meant the Fernandos would not be hurting anyone else. Also outside the court was Vester's sister Christine, thirty-six, who said he was a good bloke who had helped her care for her children. 'He wouldn't be in trouble today if he didn't drink,' she said. Apart from Professor Hayes, no one spoke up for Brendan. The Fernandos were, at the time of their conviction, the youngest people sentenced in New South Wales to spend the rest of their lives behind bars; they were also the first Aborigines to face the balance of their natural lives in gaol under the truth-in-sentencing legislation.

Issues to do with crime and punishment will always be controversial but this case, perhaps, highlights a major flaw in the law-and-order argument that a return to the death penalty and harsher sentencing overall will have the effect of reducing crime. What the Fernandos did to Sandra was undeniably monstrous and deserving of retribution, but no one can argue that, in their drink- and drug-befuddled state on the night of the murder, they were capable of considering the outcome of their actions. Had the penalty been certain — for example lingering death through being hanged, drawn and quartered — it would not have stopped them. The thought of being caught was beyond them, never mind consideration of punishment.

The challenge is for politicians to put in place long-term, effective programs that will lessen, if not remove, the social conditions that breed excessive drinking, boredom and violent crime. Had the Fernandos had some hope for their own future, they may never have cut short the life of Sandra Hoare.

Hope, however, is not always a panacea for dysfunctional individuals and families, as our next case study will show. The family around which the following chapter unfolds was widely regarded by the Australian public as a close-knit, mutually supportive unit which not only had hope for the future but which was actively taking that future, literally, into their own hands.

The story ended for Brendan Fernando on 22 September 1999 when he was found stabbed and bashed to death in the education block of the Lithgow maximum security prison. As this book went to press, his cousin Vester and another prisoner, Ronald Priestley, stood charged with his murder.

Brendan's mother, Iris, is still fighting to have her son's conviction for murder overturned and has been granted leave to appeal to the High Court. If she succeeds, the posthumous quashing of the murder conviction it will be the first in Australian legal history.

8

THE SINS OF THE FATHER

Waters and Cooper

There is no doubt that people's fascination with murder increases when the victim, perpetrator(s) or both have a high public profile, and this applies particularly if they are sporting heroes or entertainment celebrities. One of the greatest examples of this in recent years was the trial in California of OJ Simpson. The story might have been tragic but it was heaven-sent for the media since 'the Juice' as he was widely known, was something of a football legend as well as an entertainment figure, even if his stature as an actor on screen was unlikely ever to eclipse his performances on astroturf. In Australia it is often said of bizarre tales that 'these things happen only in America'. These things are, however, happening with increasing frequency here, including senseless massacres of the innocent, as happened in Hoddle Street and Queen Street, Melbourne, and in Tasmania's Port Arthur.

The scenario we look at in this chapter could itself have been dreamed up by a Hollywood scriptwriter: a sporting family acclaimed by the nation, three sons who excel in the boxing ring, and a patriarch who trains them, cares for them and nurses them to success. But wait ...

the subplot — or perhaps the main plot — in this tale is that the patriarch, in reality, is an abuser of his family, a sexual deviant and thoroughly corrupted by hatred and jealousy. The story reaches its climax as the father turns one of his sons into a brutal murderer, is charged alongside his son, but then cheats justice by succumbing to a heart attack before facing a jury of his peers.

This true story took place at Kulnara, on the central coast of New South Wales, which is noted more for its alternative lifestyles and bunny-huggers than its killers. It is a tale of tandem murder and dominance-submission, but it differs remarkably from the other cases examined in this book because it illustrates the extent to which an unscrupulous father can dominate a fearful son, using his influence to force him to commit a crime the father himself is too cowardly to attempt.

The frenzy exhibited by parents urging their children to greater efforts in sport is frequently on display at Little Athletics and Little League events. Fathers, in particular, can be consumed by the dream of seeing their children, especially sons, achieve heights in sport that they may have aspired to but could never reach. Just such a father was Cec Waters, patriarch of one of Australia's best-known boxing families. Until the truth about him emerged, Cec was seen as a tough but loving father who had guided his three sons, Dean, Troy and Guy, to every state and national title available to them, and Troy and Guy to commonwealth titles. It appeared to be one of the few father–son(s) relationships in boxing that actually worked. Fathers who elect to train their sons in boxing — and most other sports for that matter, usually fail to recognise the dividing line between coach and parent, resulting in a total breakdown of the relationship in all areas. Fathers generally lack the objectiveness to see the true capabilities of their sons, tending to either over- or under-train them. What became evident as the truth emerged in this case was that, far from being a wise and caring father, Cec Waters was monstrous. A person who instilled terror in his sons, he was a coward at heart, living out his fantasies through his three boys.

While three people were eventually charged with the murder of Allen Henry Hall at Warnervale, New South Wales, on the night of 29 June 1988, the case is included in this book on tandem murders because it is a graphic example of the dominance–submission theory. It is a little different to others, though, because in this case the dominant personality, Cec Waters, used his power over his son Dean and his co-accused Damon Ashley Cooper, a former motor mechanic turned boxer who trained at the farm, to force them to commit a murder in which he took no physical part. The outcome of the trial of Dean Waters also left open the question of whether or not a precedent has been set which will allow parental influence to be recognised as a legitimate defence in criminal trials.

Veteran Sydney crime reporter Malcolm Brown (to whom we are indebted for his research assistance) was involved with the case from the beginning. He wrote several news and features stories about it, including an in-depth feature called 'Troubled Waters' for the *Sydney Morning Herald*. Indeed, the name Waters has lent itself to a number of ambiguous titles, including the book *Raging Waters*, written by Dean with the assistance of journalist Daniel Lane and published in December 1998.

Cecil Waters emigrated to Australia in 1972 from the United Kingdom, where he had been born in 1926. He was accompanied by his wife Christine and four children — Dean, Guy, Troy and Tracy. Christine, twenty-two years his junior, was wife number four, evidence that Cec had difficulty maintaining relationships. His four children were from a previous marriage. Christine had been involved with Cec since she was seventeen and had lived with him for five years prior to their 1972 marriage. The family settled on a farm at Mangrove Mountain, where they trained horses saved from the knackery and cared for countless dogs and other stray and unwanted animals. Cec Waters, who was almost never seen without a woollen beanie perched atop his head, presented himself to the world as a fitness fanatic, totally opposed to the use of alcohol and tobacco, and dedicated to clean, healthy living. The years were kind to him, his aging face giving him the appearance of a wise, benevolent man.

A believer in order and discipline, Waters was determined that his sons would win accolades in the square ring as champion boxers, a sport that he had never had the courage to pursue himself. And so they grew up as boxers, acquitting themselves well in the amateur ranks before making their mark as professionals. Of the three brothers, Troy was by far the most talented fighter and a real world championship prospect until the tragedy of his family robbed him of his motivation. Dean and Guy did well and won substantial titles, although their talents did not compare with those of their brother Troy.

Cec Waters was smart enough to realise that he had a highly marketable commodity in his boxing family, a commodity that, for a while, the Australian media and its public could not get enough of. He enlisted the aid of former pop singer Marty Rhone and began to market the battling Waters family in earnest. This was in 1987, the year that also saw Christine leave from the family home. Earlier that year, horse wrangler and reputed drug dealer Allen Hall had arrived at the farm seeking to spar with the famous Waters brothers. Although Hall had a lengthy rap sheet for petty crime, he was welcomed into the family circle, eventually helping to train horses as well as doing some training with the boxing brothers. By this time Christine had lost interest in Cec sexually. In fact Cec actually suggested she have an affair with Hall, as a possible cure for what he saw as her frigidity. The affair eventuated; on the first night Christine and Hall made love, Cec hid behind a curtain to watch.

In December 1987 Christine left the farm to set up house at Jilliby with Hall. Cec, fearing a divorce could cost him his farm, tried to terrorise her into returning. The Jilliby house was burned down, after which Hall received a note, almost certainly written by Cec Waters, accusing him of being a worthless human being and saying there was more to come. Cec's hatred of Christine and his desire for revenge on Hall festered. Dean later alleged that, in May 1988, his father took him into Ourimbah State Forest where they dug 'holes'. Dean said Cec screamed at him that he was a coward when he walked off in disgust after being told one of the holes was to be a grave for Christine.

On the night of Allen Hall's murder, Dean and Cooper hid in bushes outside the Warnervale home Hall was sharing with Christine. Hall's dogs began to bark and when Hall emerged from the house to find out what was upsetting them, Dean opened fire with a 12-gauge shotgun and Cooper with a .22 calibre rifle. After fleeing the murder scene, they cleaned themselves up to remove incriminating evidence and disposed of the firearms.

In August 1988 Cec and Dean were charged with conspiring among themselves and others to kill Hall. Later, in October, Dean was charged with murdering Hall, and Cec with being an accessory before the fact. The following March the charges were dismissed by Magistrate Bill Pierce, who concluded that there was insufficient physical evidence to support them. It was not until eight years later, on 8 February 1996, that Dean decided he could no longer live with the truth; accompanied by his lawyer, he made a full confession to police at Gosford, New South Wales. In those intervening years, Dean and Guy had found God and Troy, the most promising boxer of the three, had fought for the world titles that appeared to be within his reach. He lost them.

Dean's confession led to the immediate arrest of

Cooper, who was tried in May of that year and convicted of manslaughter, a perplexing verdict given that the killing of Hall was clearly premeditated. It seems the jury accepted his plea that he had not been acting under his own volition but was strongly under the influence of Cec Waters. Judge Newman had no option but to accept the jury's verdict, although he showed his lack of agreement with it by sentencing Cooper to eighteen years gaol, with a minimum term of twelve years. Cooper had also pleaded guilty to burning down the Jilliby house, for which he received a further three years, to be served concurrently. Dean's confession also resulted in murder and accessory charges again being brought against him and Cec, but Cec was to escape his day in court by dying of a heart attack on 4 April.

Dean's trial blew the lid off the myth of the caring father and his devoted sons. It became a chronicle of Cec's evils and the horrific treatment he handed out to his family. The boys were debased in almost every way possible and were subjected to vicious beatings with a piece of hosepipe equipped with brass fittings. Their sister Tracy told the court that when she was just fourteen, her father had twice taken her to Sydney's infamous Kings Cross to be photographed naked with another woman. The basis of Dean's defence was that Cec had so brutalised him and his siblings that, out of sheer terror, they would do anything he demanded of them. The poignancy of his exposure of the abuse they had suffered was not lost on the jury, who found Dean not guilty of murder or manslaughter. Dean wept as the verdict was handed down.

It is not the role of this book to query the legality of any jury decision, but the Waters case does give rise to considerable speculation. As the crown prosecutor pointed out to the jury, meticulous planning had gone into the murder of Hall and the subsequent cover-up. And if, as Dean claimed, he was terrorised beyond his ability to resist carrying out Cec Waters' orders, how did he manage to choose not to kill Christine?

As we have seen in other murder cases, the dominance of a weaker partner by a stronger one is a frequent defence in cases of tandem killing. In the case of the Waters however, the dominance of a third party is being offered to explain the actions of the two perpetrators. Unquestionably, long-term dominance by a parental figure will seriously affect the life of any child, well into adulthood, but it leaves us with the most disturbing question: at what age does a person assume responsibility for his or her own actions?

It is a standard defence in many criminal cases to plead that the accused has suffered a dysfunctional, deprived childhood. In some cases this is more likely to be taken into account when the sentence is being handed down rather than at the stage when the guilt or innocence of the accused is being decided. The case of Dean Waters — and, to a lesser extent, that of Cooper — raises the question of whether a legal precedent has been set that will permit parental dominance to become a legally recognised mitigating factor in the defence of a person charged with murder or, indeed, of any crime.

Realistically, one can sympathise with Dean and his brothers and sister for their tragic upbringing, but it is difficult to accept it as a defence to murder. Perhaps it would have been easier to understand if one or all of the children had turned on Cec, then pleaded self-defence out of fear that he might one day kill one of them in one of his violent rages. Domestic violence is becoming increasingly accepted as a defence to murder, especially in the case of battered women, but it is a quantum leap of principle for this defence to be stretched to the killing of someone other than the perpetrator of the violence. It may be that the Waters case will present long-lasting headaches for prosecution and defence attorneys, not to mention judges. At the time this book was being written, Cooper's counsel, Mr Manny Conditis, was working on what he described a 'the last roll of the dice' to have his client's gaoling reviewed by the Governor of New South Wales, Sir Gordon Samuels.

Cooper's wife Julie takes their two children, twelve-year-old Amanda and nine-year-old Rhys on the 400-kilometre trip most weekends to visit him in Lithgow Gaol.

'Damon is bitter,' she told a journalist after she and the children had visited the gaol to spend Christmas Day with him in 1998. 'Dean Waters spends everyday with his children.'

9

THE EXTORTIONISTS

Stuart and Finch

On Thursday 8 March 1973, the popular Brisbane nightclub Whiskey Au Go Go, on the corner of Amelia Street and St Paul's Terrace, Fortitude Valley, resonated with the sounds of live music. The nationally successful band 'The Delltones' had finished their set by midnight, and the local group 'Trinity' took the stage to entertain the remaining patrons into the early hours of the morning. At about 2.10 am the disco atmosphere was shattered when a fire broke out in the foyer of the nightclub. Two nine-litre drums of petrol had been poured onto the carpet and ignited with a match, quickly spreading flames and lethal carbon monoxide fumes from the first floor of the two-storey building to engulf the second-level dance floor. Air-conditioning plants within the building accelerated the fire's action.

At least forty people were in the nightclub at the time the fire started, with some reports giving numbers closer to one hundred. Within the dark environment smoke and fumes reduced visibility drastically as the realisation and panic of impending disaster struck at the hearts of club patrons. Some managed to escape through a rear fire exit, while others found their escape barred by windows recently sealed to reduce neighbourhood noise complaints. A number of people were forced to smash the sealed windows and jump through the jagged glass to the footpath more than three metres below.

Intense heat and encroaching flames, combined with noxious fumes generated by burning carpet, paint and old timber, acted in synergy to asphyxiate and fatally burn those who couldn't escape. Shortly after the fire had begun, fifteen patrons lay dead in what newspapers of the time described as Australia's worst mass murder. In total five women and ten men lost their lives. Two of the victims were members of 'Trinity' one of whom was nineteen-year-old saxophonist Darcy Day. Other victims included two military police, Lesley Palethorpe and William Nolan, and the teenager Jennifer Davie, who was later to become the 'nominal victim' for the purposes of criminal proceedings against those accused of the crime.

A huge police task force was established to track down the perpetrators of the crime. Along with Queensland police, specialist police were brought in from Melbourne and Sydney to assist with the investigations. One of the New South Wales detectives was Roger Rogerson, later disgraced and charged in 1984 with conspiracy to murder undercover drug detective Michael Drury. A reward of $50 000 was offered by the Queensland government for information leading to the arrest and conviction of any offenders, with an offer of immunity from prosecution for anyone providing information who was not directly responsible for the fire.

While the special task force carried out its investigations, a maelstrom of political controversy erupted over allegations that the commonwealth police had officially warned senior Queensland police that the Whiskey Au Go Go was to be the target of a fire-bombing. Apparently one federal police officer, Bill Humphries, had forwarded the information to his Queensland counterparts two weeks before the bombing. At the time, Queensland police steadfastly denied that the warning had been given, but police foreknowledge of the bombing was later confirmed in a document tabled before the Fitzgerald Inquiry.

On 12 March, four days after the fire, Queensland police received a tip-off from Dan Stuart, implicating his brother John Stuart and James Finch in the fire-bombing. Acting on the information, police arrived at Dan's house in the western suburbs of Brisbane, where they were confronted by John Stuart wielding a large hunting knife. Initially defiant, Stuart agreed to surrender to police after a detective drew his service revolver and threatened to shoot him. Shortly after Stuart's arrest, Finch arrived at the house demanding money from Dan and his wife so he could escape from Brisbane. Police were called to the premises by the distressed couple, but Finch fled into the bushes they arrived. After a search was launched, Finch was apprehended in a nearby shopping mall by a police patrol.

James Richard Finch, twenty-eight, was born in

STUART AND FINCH

England in 1944 and placed in a children's home at the age of six after the death of his father. He was brought to Australia several years later by the Barnardo charity organisation. Growing up in a world of poverty, Finch turned to a life of petty crime. In 1965 he was convicted and sentenced to a fourteen-year gaol term for the shooting and wounding of Sydney hitman John Regan. After serving seven years of his sentence, Finch was paroled and deported back to England as an undesirable person. Stuart had brought him back to Australia a short time before the Whiskey Au Go Go fire-bombing to assist with the extortion of local nightclubs.

In contrast to Finch, John Andrew Stuart, thirty-two, was a professional criminal who was well known to Brisbane police. Originally from Sydney, he had a long list of criminal antecedents, including attempted murder. Stuart was both intelligent and attractive although, according to Malcolm Brown in his book *Australian Crime: Chilling Tales of Our Time*, he had a psychopathic personality and possibly suffered from schizophrenia. Stuart spent several of his earlier years confined in New South Wales mental institutions, and the longest stint he had spent out of prison since turned fourteen was the three months directly prior to the Whiskey Au Go Go fire-bombing.

After their arrest, Finch and Stuart were taken to the Brisbane watchhouse for questioning. Stuart refused to be interviewed or to cooperate with police in any way. Finch, however, apparently gave a tearful and full confession of his and Stuart's involvement in the fire-bombing in an unsigned record of interview typed by Detective Sergeant Ron Redmond. For reasons of speed and efficiency, both men were charged with the murder of Jennifer Denise Davie rather than with the murder of all fifteen victims.

Police alleged that Stuart and Finch were heavily involved in an extortion racket involving Brisbane nightclubs. Stuart had generated a plan to extract large sums of money from nightclub owners in return for guaranteed protection of their premises, and had paid the $600 airfare to bring Finch out from England to aid him in these activities. Having rejected the pair's demands for money, the Whiskey Au Go Go nightclub was chosen as a suitable target to fire-bomb in an attempt to scare other club owners into complying with their demands. While Finch was lighting the fire, Stuart was careful to make his presence known at the Flamingo nightclub in order to secure an alibi for the time of the fire-bombing. In the lead-up to the offence, and to add further weight to his alibi, Stuart had informed local newspapers that criminals from Sydney had penetrated the Brisbane nightclub scene and that a nightclub was going to be fire-bombed as a result.

After they were charged, Stuart and Finch were remanded in custody until their hearing before the Brisbane Magistrates Court. At the hearing, the pair protested their innocence, arguing that they had been 'verballed' by the police. To be 'verballed' is an expression which grew out of the police practice of stating in court that the accused 'made certain verbal admissions to me'. Unquestionably, there have been occasions when police, no doubt working on the principle that a suspect may not be guilty of the alleged crime but is certainly guilty of something, have fabricated these so-called verbal admissions. Over the years, nonetheless, it became a standard defence ploy for an accused person to claim that he or she had been 'verballed'.

In the case of Stuart and Finch, they entered pleas of not guilty and were detained in the high security wing of Queensland's notorious Boggo Road gaol until a number of preliminary hearings had taken place. During this period, Finch and Stuart continued to argue their innocence and to accuse police of fabricating the unsigned record of interview. At this point their protests began to include a variety of self-injurious behaviours. Finch apparently gnawed off the top of his little finger with his teeth in protest against the police 'set-up'. Recent evidence, however, suggests that the finger was probably severed with some sort of cutting instrument, possibly a razor blade.

Both Finch and Stuart also began the practice of swallowing wire crosses which they had constructed in their cells. These crosses, which had sharp ends, became lodged in their digestive tracts shortly after ingestion. Finch was operated on at the security wing of the Royal Brisbane Hospital to remove the crosses, and this experience apparently motivated him to desist from further indulgence in the habit. Despite surgical intervention, Stuart continued to ingest metal objects well after Finch had stopped. Although Stuart's behaviour was an attempt to delay proceedings for as long as possible, the trial went ahead in his absence.

In October 1973 the Supreme Court of Queensland found Finch and Stuart guilty of the murder of Jennifer Davie, and both were sentenced to life imprisonment. Although Stuart had generated an alibi for himself, he was deemed by the court to be an equal party to the crime as he had developed the plan and commissioned Finch to carry it out. The pair were convicted on the basis of Finch's unsigned record of interview, as well as the evidence of a convicted rapist, Arthur Murdock. Murdock had told the Supreme Court that Finch had confessed to him in gaol while they were sharing the same cell although, in one of the many twists to the Whiskey Au Go Go tale, Murdock later claimed that he had been forced to concoct Finch's confession by gaol Superintendent Roy Stephenson. This was revealed in a record of interview made by Murdock on 23 June 1977, which outlined how he had been paid $1000 for fabricating the confession.

Maintaining their innocence, Finch and Stuart appealed against their sentences several times, with Finch taking the matter all the way to the Privy Council. Each appeal was, however, systematically rejected. Finch settled into life at Boggo Road gaol reasonably well, despite the fact that he viewed his imprisonment as an injustice.

STUART AND FINCH

Stuart was not so complacent. He embarked on an aggressive campaign against the prison system, for example, at times spitting and hurling excrement at prison warders who attended his cell. This behaviour eventually caused prison authorities to secure him within a special section of the prison, isolated from other inmates.

At one stage Stuart managed to break away from an escort and climb onto the roof of one of the prison wings. While there, he tore up the iron guttering and hurled it into the compound, as well as spelling out the words 'Innocent. Victim of police verballing' using bricks from the roof. He was later to say to the media: 'Me! The wire-eating, sewage-hurling, roof-climbing, press depicted caged and spitting monster of Boggo Road, what hope have I of redress, of justice?' On New Year's Day 1980, Stuart was found dead in his cell at the age of thirty-eight. An autopsy revealed that he had died of a heart-related problem and that there was no evidence of foul play. Despite these findings, however, Stuart's mother and a number of fellow inmates maintained that he was murdered.

In stark contrast to Stuart, Finch became a model prisoner. Stating that he wouldn't eat anything that had been killed, he also became a vegetarian as well as a fitness fanatic who undertook a gruelling daily workout that lasted for up to three hours. Finch also adopted a new philosophy on life, becoming a born-again Christian. He later earned the nickname 'Birdman of Boggo Road', after being given responsibility for maintaining the gaol aviary. He also cared for any sick or injured birds found within the confines of the prison, as well as keeping a number of pet birds in his cell. He was first allowed this privilege when a local politician, Kevin Hooper, gave him a gift of a budgerigar.

In November 1983 Finch cemented his image as a model prisoner when he refused to take part in massive riots within Boggo Road gaol. His cell was one of the few not wrecked by the rioters. He prevented the rioting inmates from setting fire to the buildings, and helped prison authorities negotiate an end to the unrest. He also became a prolific letter writer, corresponding on a daily basis with anyone who might help his cause. Aided by his good behaviour and his continual claims of innocence, Finch began to attract sympathy from many outside the prison system. Journalists, human rights activists and legal experts began to openly voice their support.

One activist group, the Plea For Justice Committee, believed Finch was a victim of a blatant miscarriage of justice, and gave him the same support that they had given to Lindy Chamberlain over the death of her baby, Azaria. Adopting the name 'Friends of Finch', they sent numerous letters to the media, police and politicians, demanding his release. Lindy Chamberlain went so far as to issue a statement through her solicitor calling for an inquiry into the Whiskey Au Go Go matter and Finch's claims of innocence. Chamberlain apparently felt empathy for Finch's cause, acknowledging the many parallels between the two cases.

In 1983 a supporter by the name of Cheryl Cole was introduced to Finch by a former friend of Stuart. Cheryl, thirty-four, began corresponding with Finch in gaol, quickly developing a strong relationship with him. Confined to a wheelchair as a result of a fatal genetic disease, Cheryl became Finch's greatest supporter. Eventually the pair fell in love and, after a number of appeals to prison authorities, were married in 1986 in a historic prison wedding.

In that same year, evidence that Finch had been verballed in his unsigned confession came in an unusual form. A Scottish linguist, Reverend Andrew Q Morton, raised serious doubts about the authenticity of the alleged confession. Morton was the leading exponent of a scientific technique called stylometry, which was a method for identifying the author of written material by examining the frequency and placement of particular words. He had gained considerable credibility in British courts, where the science of stylometry had been accepted in a number of cases involving alleged police verballing. According to reports at the time, after Morton's first appearance in court, Scotland Yard's administrators issued a directive to their detectives to 'resist any temptation to verbal suspects, as verballing can now be detected'.

Morton had been brought to Australia with the assistance of the Friends of Finch organisation, with the hope of providing enough leverage for Finch to secure an appeal and an eventual release. After carrying out a detailed stylometric analysis of the 'record of interview' which facilitated the conviction of Finch, Morton declared that the mathematical probability of Finch having composed the confession was 236 472 to 1. This evidence was put before a number of Queensland authorities, including the Attorney General, but was ultimately dismissed. As a result, Finch's ninth appeal for a retrial was rejected by the governor, Sir Walter Campbell, based on advice given to him from the Crown Law Department. Ron Redmond, who had typed Finch's unsigned record of interview and was by then Assistant Police Commissioner, obviously viewed the latest evidence as a personal attack. He went so far as to issue a writ against Morton for having made the accusations.

Largely through the efforts of Cheryl and the Friends of Finch organisation, the Queensland government granted Finch parole on 16 February 1988. Having served fourteen years and nine months of his life sentence, he was granted parole on the condition of immediate deportation back to England. He was subsequently released from Boggo Road and escorted by police to Brisbane airport. Due to her illness, Cheryl Finch was unable to accompany her husband to England, and the couple spent a few brief moments together at the airport before his departure. As he boarded his deportation flight from Brisbane, Finch gave the V for victory sign and exclaimed: 'I'll be back to tell the truth . . . if I'm allowed to.'

In England, Finch was given a chilly reception. The

local media were not very accommodating when it came to the repatriation of one of their more infamous nationals. The *Daily Mirror* headline read 'Welcome Home Killer', and carried with it comments from angry members of the British parliament objecting to Finch's re-entry into England. After receiving medical clearance and raising money through public donations for her airfare, Cheryl followed Finch to London. But within three months she had left him and returned to Brisbane, apparently because the cold English conditions aggravated her condition. Unfortunately for Cheryl, Finch had also turned out to be an abusive husband.

In 1988, after declaring his innocence for fifteen years, Finch had an incredible statement to make to the Australian media. In an interview with Denis Watt, a reporter for the *Sun*, Finch confessed to his and Stuart's part in the Whiskey Au Go Go fire-bombing. He also implicated Robert McCulkin, who he identified as having driven the getaway car; the criminal Vincent O'Dempsey, who had planned the bombing; and Thomas Hamilton, who assisted him in lighting the fire. Finch quickly withdrew his confession, however, when it was suggested by Queensland authorities that he could be extradited for the murders of the other fourteen victims. After Finch had made his confession, Cheryl responded to newspapers that the confession was all lies, and that her husband's mental instability, confusion and loneliness were to blame for his actions.

In that same year the *Courier Mail* interviewed John

Stuart's brother Dan, who had been in hiding under police protection in Cairns since giving evidence at the trial. Dan confirmed that Stuart and Finch were responsible for the fire. He told the newspaper that on the night of the fire-bombing, his brother and Finch had asked him for a fuel drum, which he had supplied to them without question. Dan also produced a number of letters, written by John Stuart and Finch prior to the fire-bombing, that detailed the proposed extortion of Brisbane nightclubs. When he heard about Dan Stuart's testimony, Finch responded from England alleging that the story was fabricated and that Dan had been paid to tell it by the Queensland police.

Despite Finch's confession and his apparent contribution to the Whiskey Au Go Go murders, controversy still surrounded the unsigned record of interview that had secured the 1973 conviction. The Fitzgerald Inquiry into Police Corruption only added to the debate. Before the inquiry, a corrupt former police officer, Jack Herbert, admitted that verballing was common within the Queensland police service. It was also revealed that police were involved in protection rackets within the Fortitude Valley area at the time of the Whiskey Au Go Go fire-bombing. In an interesting twist, a secret police document, tabled before the Fitzgerald Inquiry, indicated that Stuart was a police informant who had spied on Queensland police suspected of corruption. The Queensland police were highly factionalised at the time of the fire-bombing, and Stuart was not popular among some of those factions.

In 1988 two unidentified police officers told the ABC 'Four Corners' program that Finch had been verballed by investigating police. At the same time, one of the six detectives involved in the interview of Finch anonymously admitted to Bruce Stannard of the *Bulletin* that Finch's confession had been falsely generated, and that Finch had been physically beaten. Police were apparently certain of the guilt of Finch and Stuart, and had subsequently verballed Finch to ensure a conviction.

Although the police were later supported in their assumption of Finch's guilt, the question of verballing raises serious questions about police practices at the time. This activity, at times referred to as 'noble cause corruption', involves acts of corruption designed for the greater good of society rather than for any personal gain on the part of the police officer. There are a number of reasons for this particular corrupt practice, not the least of which is the frustration police may encounter with the legal system itself when offenders are released on procedural or evidentiary technicalities. Despite any apparent 'noble' ambitions, though, it is not sufficient within our legal system for police to 'know' that a person is guilty and then to ignore established legal guidelines to ensure a subsequent conviction. To do so can only serve to jeopardise the entire criminal justice system.

In the case of the Whiskey Au Go Go fire-bombing,

both the media and public alike demanded a quick police response. Queensland politicians saw the case as a test of police proficiency and prestige. These pressures acted together to encourage the over-zealous police response which resulted in years of controversy and criticism.

Clearly, the Whiskey Au Go Go case is markedly different from other forms of tandem murder. This was a predatory crime carried out by two semi-professional criminals with the object of extorting money from nightclubs. The enormous public sympathy accorded to Finch would never have occurred — regardless of the allegations of 'verballing' or the offender's alleged rehabilitation — if the killings had had hedonistic sexual overtones like the majority of cases discussed in this book. Crime, however, even in its most petty form, has been the prime motivation for other tandem murders, as we shall see in our next chapter when we recount how two people died over the division of paltry profits resulting from deals in stolen lawnmowers.

10

KILLING FOR BUSINESS

Peckman and Peckman

The dreamscape imagination of author Stephen King created a virtual reality monster in his short story 'The Lawnmower Man', which was later to become, as they say in Hollywood, 'a major motion picture'. The question of whether art mirrors life or life mirrors art is contentious; certainly it is extremely doubtful that King had ever heard of Melbourne axe murderer Harold Peckman. What is almost certain is that, if Peckman had committed his crimes twenty years later, the media, riding on the back of King's genius, would have dubbed him 'The Lawnmower Man'. Personal monetary gain, especially when dealing with business partners, is a well-understood motive for murder. But in 1970 when Peckman, then thirty-two, stood trial for the brutal murders of Albert Taylor, also thirty-two, and his pregnant wife Kathleen Pearl Taylor, twenty-eight, it was difficult to believe he had been motivated by the pittance involved in a stolen lawnmower business.

Harold Peckman, at the time of his trial, was a darkly good-looking young man of twenty-eight, well-muscled and lean, and of medium height. He wore his wavy brown hair short. Although he committed the murders alone, we have included him in this book because of the influence he exerted over his brother, Neville John Peckman, who was twenty-seven at the time he stood trial. Harold had tried to get his younger brother to help dispose of the savagely mutilated bodies, and the initial police investigation was hampered when each of the brothers accused the other of the killings. The Peckman case is an example of one person influencing the other — despite the fact that, in this case, the influence did not appear to be powerful — in order to engage in murder.

There was evidence that the brothers had been separated as children following the breakdown of their family. It was not explained how they found each other again but they did so shortly before Harold murdered the Taylors. What did emerge was that Neville took fraternal loyalty far more seriously than Harold: while Neville was prepared to help his brother try to cover up the grisly crime, Harold blatantly accused Neville of being the killer after their arrest.

About two years earlier, in 1968, Peckman had formed a business association with the Taylors. The arrangement was quite simple. Peckman and Albert Taylor cruised Melbourne's grassy suburbs stealing motorised lawnmowers. They took them back to the Taylors' rented home in the inner suburb of St Kilda, where Kathleen Taylor cleaned and, if necessary, painted the mowers, which then were sold on the secondhand market. Whatever the trio managed to make out of the enterprise was split equally between them. After a time Taylor decided that, since they were using his car and his wife was cleaning up the stolen goods for sale, he should get a bigger cut. What he did not realise was just how big a 'cut' he and his wife would get from Peckman.

Peckman actually went on trial twice. His first trial was aborted by the then Chief Justice of Victoria, Sir Henry Winneke, when the judge, Mr Justice Lush, became seriously ill. A month later, in December 1970, Peckman stood trial before Mr Justice Anderson. One of the most telling witnesses against Peckman was George Campbell, a fifty-year-old man he had become friendly with in the remand yard of Pentridge Prison. It was not revealed at his trial why Peckman had been on remand, no doubt because this could have prejudiced the jury against him but it is unlikely that it had anything to do with the deaths of the Taylors. He had approached Campbell asking him to arrange bail for himself and Peckman would have known that at that time bail was never granted in capital cases. Campbell told the court he had a reputation as a 'fixer' but said he told Peckman that at that stage he was not even able to arrange bail for himself. The reason Peckman gave for the urgency of his request was that he had murdered two people and buried their bodies in a shallow grave near the Gippsland city of Sale. He was concerned because the bodies had been in his car for some time before being buried and a leg of one of them had been sticking out 'at an awkward angle'. Campbell said

Peckman feared the bodies could easily be discovered.

Over a few days, during their exercise periods in the yard, Peckman told Campbell the macabre tale of his killing of the Taylors, sparing not even the most gruesome details. The court was told that on the night of 6 November 1968, Peckman entered the Taylors' apartment in Spencer Street, St Kilda, by removing glass louvres from the bathroom window. He hid inside the apartment until everyone there had gone to bed, then made his way to the main bedroom.

Campbell said Peckman had told him the couple had three children who were trained 'never to come out of their bedroom under any circumstances'. The children were aged five, three and a half, and eighteen months. He also said Peckman had expected to find Albert Taylor sleeping alone because of alleged marital problems between the couple. In the bedroom, he found Albert and another person, whom he believed to be a man, sharing the double bed. He referred to Albert as the 'small man' and the other person as 'the big man'. It evolved that 'the big man' was, in fact, Kathleen Taylor, who was heavily pregnant at the time of her slaying.

Although dubbed 'the axe murderer' by the media, the weapon actually used by Peckman was a tomahawk of the type used for cutting kindling wood. The story he was alleged to have told Campbell was that he went into the bedroom and hit Albert Taylor across the face and throat with the tomahawk, apparently killing him instantly. As Campbell told the court: 'He was dead, no trouble. He turned to the bigger man [Mrs Taylor] and hit him across the face the same way but it didn't kill him. He said he smashed and smashed at the head. He then struck across the throat but still couldn't stop him breathing. He said he attacked the chest and made a great wound but the person was still breathing.'

Peckman attacked his second victim for more than an hour with the tomahawk and a kitchen knife before the person died, said Campbell, adding: 'By this time the place was like a shambles'. In one version of the evidence given at the trial, Peckman was alleged to have reversed the tomahawk and used the blunt end of the blade to smash a gaping hole in Mrs Taylor's chest. Seeing her heart still beating, he went to the kitchen where he found an old bayonet, he took hold of her heart and used the bayonet to saw it in half.

Predictably, the bedroom was blood-soaked. After the killings, Peckman pushed a kitchen table across the doorway of the children's room to stop them getting out. Campbell said Peckman told him he would have been forced to kill the children as well if they had emerged. After cleaning up the room as best he could, Peckman put the blood-soaked mattress and some of the Taylors' belongings into his car. His brother, Neville, told the court Peckman woke him in the early hours of the morning at the apartment the brothers shared with Peckman's de facto wife Jenny Logan.

Neville said Peckman told him he had killed the Taylors

and needed assistance to get rid of the bodies. Cross-examined by Peckman's barrister, Mr Col McLeod, Neville denied he had killed the Taylors. Pointing at his brother in the dock, Neville said: 'I didn't do it. He did.' This was the only time during his trial that Harold Peckman showed any emotion. He reacted to the accusation by jumping to his feet and shouting so incoherently at Neville that he had to be restrained by a prison officer. In fact one of this book's authors covered the trial for a metropolitan newspaper and commented in his reports that Peckman seemed devoid of emotion, even when the most grisly of his actions were being described in detail to the jury.

Peckman took Neville with him back to the Taylors' apartment. They found a large plastic wrapper from a mattress and used it to wrap the bodies which they then loaded into the rear seat of Peckman's car, covering them with blankets. The plan was to take them out into the country and bury them. But Peckman's sense of direction led to a delay. Taking the wrong turn on Melbourne's major highway, Dandenong Road, the brothers ended up on Beach Road. They decided it was getting too close to daylight to continue with their plan to dispose of the Taylors, so they drove back home and parked the car. The bodies were left in the car on a South Melbourne street all day.

The following evening, the brothers returned to the car to find that nature was taking its course. The bodies had begun to deteriorate and smelled quite badly. Peckman sprinkled them with after-shave lotion in an effort to keep the smell of death at bay. Campbell said that Peckman had told him that he had never been able to stand the smell of aftershave lotion since. Eventually the bodies were buried, along with the mattress and the Taylors' belongings, in a shallow grave.

Neville's barrister, Mr McLeod, introduced into evidence a letter which Neville admitted writing, although he said he had done so only at Peckman's request. The letter, written to Jenny Logan, was reproduced in full in *Melbourne Truth* newspaper after the trial. It was written in poor English, with many mistakes and the writer referred to Albert Taylor as 'Allen', which may have been the name Albert was know by, or an assumption on Neville's part if Albert had generally been reffered to as merely 'Al'. *Truth* published it verbatim but for the purposes of this book we have corrected many of the original errors. The letter read:

Dear Jen,
I know you don't think much of myself for what I have done to you and Hal [Harold Peckman]. But I have got to explain to you how it was and why I haven't said anything before now. It all started the night I saw someone at Hal's car when we were living in Elsternwick.

I followed him and saw him with Allen and his wife [the Taylors] and after finding out that they had cut Hal's brake hose on the car I decided to do something to their car the next night, anyway they went home when I went over there and got into their house through the bathroom window, they had tons of stuff in the house, I was going to knock it off but I heard someone and got scared and got out and I had an axe and an army bayonet to use on their car but I hid it in the house.

I went across the next night after Col [Neville's wife was named Colleen] had fallen asleep, their car wasn't there so I was going to get in and take their stuff they had.

But when I got in Jen there wasn't hardly anything. I then got the axe and bayonet and was going to take all that was left.

I knew the kids might have been in their room so I went as quiet as I could so I wouldn't wake the kids. I went into Allen's [Taylor's] room to see if there was anything there I could take, I hadn't turned the lights on and their room was dark.

I was sure that the room was empty and when I fell over an ashtray on a stand I landed on the bed. Jen next thing I knew someone jumped up and I swung at me with the axe and there was someone else grabbing at me. I hit them with the axe or bayonet I'm not sure but I kept hitting until they fell away from me.

Jen I didn't realise what I had done to them until it was over I didn't even think that I had killed them with the axe and bayonet until I saw them in my hand if there was ever a time I wanted to die that was it.

I spewed my guts up and couldn't help feeling sick I had killed them both Jen and I can say this much if I had two feathers in my hands I would still have swung at those two because I just panicked.

Well Jen after a while I calmed down a bit and decided I had to do something with them so I rolled them up in blankets and sheets and put them in my car and then I went back and cleaned up the place I had to turn the lights on and God it was mess all their personal gear I put in the car and then I came back home.

I don't know what time it was but I heard the milky on his run and when I got back home I came around the back to get in. Hal was in the kitchen and I told him I needed his help to get rid of them.

We could only get rid of the mattress before it was too light and we had to come home, we parked the car a couple of blocks away and that's why I said the car was at the service station getting repairs so you and Col wouldn't wake up to me.

That night we went and bunged them up near Sale.

Jen when the police picked me up in Adelaide and told me Hal said he did it I was scared again and went along with them. I couldn't understand why he said he did it but at the time I wasn't going to say anything. I only thought of my own skin and when I heard him tell you he has pleaded guilty all along I shut up and said no more because I wanted to make sure I wasn't the one but now you all know what happened. I can't face Col and feel proud or you and Hal so I have to stand up and face what I deserve.

I'm a weak person when it comes to facing the truth. I don't think I have ever grown up and God Jen if you hate me and I knew Hal wasn't going to say anything

> *against me because he's a man, how do you think I feel knowing how low I have sunk.*
>
> *What hurts me most is what I have done to Col. She's so young and to be 'chagd' down with me at her age I cannot be forgiven.*
>
> *So Jen forgive me if you can for hurting you and Hal.*
>
> *Neville.*

The reference in the letter to Peckman pleading guilty all along should not be taken literally. Neville, whether he wrote the letter on his volition in an attempt to confuse the police or at his brother's behest, would have meant simply that Peckman was taking the blame. Since the death penalty was still mandatory in Victoria at that time, anyone charged with murder was required by law to plead 'not guilty'.

When Peckman gave evidence for himself, he accused Neville of committing the murders. He claimed he was the one who had been at home sleeping and that Neville had woken him to help dispose of the bodies. He even said that the details in the story he told Campbell had come from Neville talking incessantly on that night and from his own observations when he accompanied his brother to the Taylors' apartment. Peckman assured the court that he never meant to divulge his brother's crime but said he had no alternative once he himself had been charged with the murders. His apparent reticence to accuse his brother did nothing to sway the jury of five women and seven men, who chose to believe police evidence that Neville was far too vague on many details to have been the actual killer. After deliberating for five hours, the jury found Harold Peckman guilty on both counts of murder. He shook his head in disagreement as the verdicts were read out.

As was required by the State of Victoria at that time, Mr Justice Anderson donned the black cap and sentenced Peckman to death. Peckman's reaction was simply to say: 'I don't believe it. I'm against capital punishment.' No doubt the Taylors would have agreed with him had they had the chance. Neville Peckman had earlier been sentenced to five years' imprisonment for his part in the disposal of the Taylors' bodies.

Harold Peckman's death sentence was eventually commuted to forty years' imprisonment and he faded from the public eye, coming back into the spotlight briefly on four occasions. The first was on 3 October 1972 when he tried to escape from prison but was foiled. The following February, Peckman was more successful in escaping from Pentridge. He caused a flurry of media warnings that a notorious axe murderer was on the loose but he was back in custody within one day, having harmed no one and disappointing the media with the briefness of his taste of freedom.

Then, in November 1989, the media took umbrage that prisoners from Morwell River prison, a low security facility not all that far from the place where Peckman had buried the Taylors twenty-one years earlier, were to present performances of the David Williamson play *The Club* before audiences of children at Traralgon and Morwell high schools. Peckman was included in the cast and the play was directed by Keith Ryrie, who had been sentenced to death in 1966 for the horrific sex murder of five-year-old Rhonda Irwin. Almost certainly the public outcry against the 1967 hanging of Ronald Ryan, the last person in Australia to be legally executed, influenced the then premier of Victoria, Sir Henry Bolte, known widely as 'Hanging Henry' to commute Ryrie's death sentence within weeks of Ryan's final drop. Ryrie was sentenced to fifty years.

Peckman made the news once more when he was freed from prison on 14 August 1992, just two days after having successfully petitioned for a minimum term under the 1991 Sentencing Act. He was awarded a minimum term of fifteen years, which was largely academic since he already had served twenty-one years.

It is difficult to neatly categorise the Peckman murders. On the surface this killing could be classified as a predatory one, although the horrific way in which Mrs Taylor was murdered indicated an almost pathological desire to ensure that the woman was, in fact, dead. Unlike the perpretrators in Whiskey Au Go Go case, neither of the Peckmans could be called professional — or even semi-professional — criminals. These were murders borne out of peculiar personal differences rather than from a long-term obsession with violence or sexual gratification.

Although Neville Peckman was not involved in the murder of the Taylors, his apparent willingness to help in the disposal of the bodies indicated that his brother did not have to exert a great deal of pressure on him in order to gain his cooperation. It was only when the two were charged with the crimes that animosity between them set in, with each blaming the other. As we have seen in other chapters, this is a not uncommon phenomenon among tandem killers. But it is not only the division of spoils that disrupts honour among thieves. Indeed, perhaps the most compelling motivation for murder among criminals is fear — fear of being caught; fear of other, more powerful criminals; fear that can unleash a chain reaction of violent death.

11

KILLING IN THE UNDERWORLD

Wright and Haigh

One of the most dreadful murders in Australian criminal history was perpetrated on a man who himself had killed his way to notoriety as a violent criminal. Barry Robert Quinn was thirty-six when, in July 1984, a fellow inmate of Jika Jika, the infamous maximum security section of Victoria's Pentridge prison, poured industrial glue over him and set him on fire.

In a carefully orchestrated attack in the hobby and craft room, apparently unseen by any prison officers, a container of the highly volatile glue was tipped over Quinn and — with the taunt, 'Here, catch this,' — a lighted match was flicked at him. His clothing flared like a torch. Before prison officers could reach him, he had suffered third-degree burns to at least eighty per cent of his body. Quinn, the man who during his short life had been the catalyst for at least seven murders, was rushed to Melbourne's Alfred Hospital where he took about six hours to die. Alekos Taikmaskis was convicted of murdering him in 1984.

Police were later to say that Quinn's last statement was a denial that he had killed any of the seven people to whose deaths he was linked. Included in his denial was the March 1974 double murder at a St Kilda motel which had landed Quinn a life sentence in gaol.

When writing about murder in Australia it is almost obligatory to bring up Quinn's name somewhere, but the reason for his inclusion in this work on tandem murders really concerns his friends and fellow convicted killers Robert Lindsay Wright and Paul Steven Haigh. Wright and Haigh were charged with committing four murders as partners. Unlike most tandem killers, it appears they shared no intense personal relationship and there were no obvious elements of sexual motivation or thrill killing involved in their crimes. Habitual criminals, the pair killed to silence witnesses, initially on behalf of their friend Quinn but later out of what they saw as self-preservation. Like ripples in a pond, each killing involved another potential witness who needed to be removed.

Any examination of the murders for which Wright and Haigh stood trial cannot be carried out without including Quinn. Although he was acquitted at the trial which gaoled Wright and Haigh, Quinn, unquestionably provided the motivation for the killings. So, since the story of Wright and Haigh is inextricably interwoven with that of Quinn, it is necessary to first look at the events that drew them into this web of murder.

The list of players in this story is a long one:

- Drago Pukar and Josip Slokar were victims in the double slaying at the Car-O-Tel motel, 1974: Barry Quinn was charged with their murder.
- Ivanka Katherine Karlson, better known as Eva, was killed at Mississippi Creek, near Warburton, 1978: Quinn and Wright were charged with her murder.
- Wayne Keith Smith, small-time drug dealer, was killed at St Kilda, 1979: Wright and Haigh were charged with his murder.
- Sheryle Gardner and her nine-year-old son Danny Mitchell were murdered at Ripponlea, 1979: Wright and Haigh were charged with their murder.
- Lisa Brearley was murdered in the Olinda State Forest, 1979: Wright and Haigh were charged with her murder.

The story of the charges and the sequence of events follows, beginning with the crime which led to this series of deaths and its key perpetrator — Barry Quinn.

Quinn's family home was at Braybrook, in Melbourne's predominantly blue-collar western suburbs, but he seems to have spent little time there. Before his leap to prominence as a double murderer, he had drifted from one small-time criminal act to another, amassing a substantial running sheet of minor crime. While it could be argued that at the time $100 was a tangible sum of money, few people would have considered it sufficient to warrant the taking of two lives. Yet, on 25 March 1974, Quinn shot dead two men for just that sum.

At his trial Quinn was convicted on overwhelming evidence and sentenced to life in prison, despite his deathbed claims that he was innocent. His victims were Drago Pukar, thirty-four, and Josip Slokar, thirty-three, who were behind the reception desk of the motel when Quinn burst in and killed them with a .410 shotgun. It was never suggested there was any motive for the murders other than robbery. The conviction and sentencing of Quinn was to cause the violent death of three women, one man and a nine-year-old boy in an apparently systematic extermination of witnesses. Ironically, two of the women had been Quinn's lovers. The nine-year-old boy's only crime was to have been born at the wrong time and in the wrong circumstances.

After Quinn's conviction on the Car-O-Tel murders, he was taken to Pentridge prison, where he remained until November 1978. Complaining of illness, Quinn saw the prison medical staff and was diagnosed as having hepatitis. Hepatitis is highly contagious and could have caused major problems in the crowded prison so, in the interests of his own health and that of his fellow inmates, Quinn was transferred under security to Fairfield Infectious Diseases Hospital. On 15 November, with the help of Eva Karlson, Robert Wright and Wayne Keith Smith, Quinn escaped from the hospital. After remaining at large for little more than two months, he was recaptured in Perth in the company of his girlfriend, Sheryle Ann Gardner.

Photographs of Quinn taken after his recapture in January 1979 showed him with flowing, shoulder-length dark hair and a full beard and moustache. His sharp features and piercing eyes — together with the media's penchant for never missing an opportunity — led to him being likened to US cult-leader killer Charles Manson. Indeed, the trail of death leading to the 1980 trial of Quinn, Wright and Haigh strongly indicated that Quinn engendered in his associates a fanatical loyalty not unlike that shown to Manson by his minions.

In September 1980 Quinn, Wright and Haigh stood trial in the Supreme Court of Victoria on a variety of charges. They were tried together because their alleged crimes were all part of the same scenario. Quinn and Wright were charged with having murdered Ivanka Katherine (Eva) Karlson at Mississippi Creek, near Warburton, between 16 November 1978 and 30 July 1979. (The prosecution based these dates on the last time Karlson was known to be alive and the discovery of her badly decomposed remains. Although Quinn was back in custody in January 1979 and the evidence indicated Karlson had been killed soon after his escape, the uncertainty surrounding the date of her death no doubt contributed to his acquittal of her murder.) Wright and Haigh were charged with the murders of Wayne Keith Smith at St Kilda on 27 June 1979, Sheryle Ann Gardner and Danny Mitchell at Ripponlea on or about 22 July 1979, and Lisa Brearley at the Olinda State Forest on or about 8 August 1979.

William O'Connor, an unemployed man who admitted to the court he was a confidence trickster, told of meeting Wright and Haigh in a Springvale hotel on 14 July 1979. He accepted an invitation from Wright to spend the night at Wright's home in the beachside suburb of Edithvale. The following day he went with Wright and Haigh to the St Kilda apartment of Lisa Brearley, Haigh's nineteen-year-old girlfriend who he wanted to 'bite' for some money, O'Connor said. He heard Wright say to Haigh: 'You can't trust sheilas ... should have got rid of her.' O'Connor said that later he was 'astounded' when Wright asked him to drive a car for Haigh and himself 'so we can get rid of a few people'. O'Connor claimed to have refused, saying: 'That's not my go ... that's not my cup of tea.'

But the most damning evidence was given by key witness Ernest Reginald Strachan, a twenty-three-year-old known associate of the three killers. In fact Strachan, from the Melbourne suburb of Clayton, admitted being present during two of the murders. First to die after Quinn's escape was Eva Karlson, the woman who had helped him evade two prison officers at Fairfield Hospital and driven him away in a car, ironically, to join Quinn's 'official' girlfriend, Sheryle Gardner. Quinn was whisked away to a campsite near Warburton, in hilly country to Melbourne's east. The court was told that before being sentenced to life in gaol, Quinn had lived with Gardner but had carried on a secret affair with Karlson. After his escape he lived at the campsite with Karlson until, around the end of November, Gardner came visiting in the company of Wright. It seems Karlson was then shot dead, and there was evidence that Gardner was present at the time. At this point of his life

Quinn had virtually nothing to lose. He already was under a life sentence, so even recapture and conviction for further crimes would in reality add nothing to his gaol time. The worst it could do would be to slow down the likelihood of his parole at some date well into the future.

Based on evidence given at their trial, the most probable trigger for the events that followed was that Wright, in particular, became fearful of there being too many walking and potentially talking people who knew of his involvement with Quinn, and now of Karlson's murder. Among those who knew too much was Wayne Smith. On 27 June 1979 Wright and Haigh, in the company of Ernest Strachan, went to premises in St Kilda occupied by Smith. Strachan claimed to have waited outside and heard gunshots. Another mouth was closed.

Lisa Brearley was technically a 'cleanskin' although she was heavily involved with the criminal element. This meant she was able to legally apply for and receive a shooter's permit through her local police station. Armed with the permit, she and Wright went shopping and bought two .22 calibre rifles. Some five days later, Sheryle Gardner and her son Danny were sitting in her car drinking milkshakes in the affluent suburb of Ripponlea when they were murdered in a hail of bullets. Within a week or so, there was word on the street that police were seeking a young woman named Lisa who had used her shooter's licence to purchase two rifles. The rumour was to cost Brearley her life.

It was Strachan who told the court how Brearley was disposed of. On the night in question, Haigh apparently told Strachan that the four of them — Strachan, Wright, Haigh and Brearley — were going to a party in the Dandenongs. Strachan said he drove them all in Brearley's car. Tempers became frayed when the car bogged down on a mountain bush track. In one ear Strachan had Wright telling him to drive it out and, in the other, Brearley yelling at him because he was 'thrashing' the engine. Strachan then claimed Haigh had 'done his nut' and grabbed Brearley, who appealed to Strachan to 'tell them I ain't done nothing'. Strachan alleged that after the four got out of the car, Haigh had thrown Brearley to the ground and Wright told Strachan to get back into the car.

He thought he saw a knife in Haigh's hand, Strachan said, adding: 'He had done something to her because she made a terrible sound . . . a sort of gargling, gurgling.' When he asked Wright what had happened, Wright told him: 'Keep cool and don't get paranoid, or you go down with us.' Strachan admitted he helped Haigh drag Brearley's body along a bush track and cover it with bark and bracken. Crown prosecutor Mr Gordon Taylor told the jury that Brearley had been stabbed 157 times. The dead woman's car was taken to Lilydale train station and wiped to remove fingerprints.

Wright was represented by distinguished silk Mr John Phillips QC, later to become a Supreme Court Justice and, eventually, Chief Justice of Victoria. Mr Phillips was known to do his homework well and to be articulate and relentless in cross-examination. Phillips had Strachan agree that whoever killed Brearley had gone 'berserk', then asked Strachan if that was not a condition he regularly got into himself. Strachan denied it. Mr Phillips went on to get admissions from Strachan that he was a heavy drinker and a spasmodic user of heroin and LSD. Strachan said he drank an average of ten bottles of beer each day, had sniffed or injected heroin and had 'tripped' on LSD on, perhaps, five occasions. He also admitted he could be violent towards women but 'only when they need it'.

For some three years from 1976 Strachan had lived with Wright's sister, Mr Phillips said, and had once 'had a blue' with her when she was in the advanced stages of pregnancy. Strachan said he had had several 'blues' with her. 'And you threw a full bottle at her stomach, didn't you?' accused Mr Phillips. Strachan denied this, saying that he had, in fact, thrown a half-empty bottle at her head.

Haigh's counsel, Mr Boris Kayser, also attacked Strachan relentlessly, accusing him of perjuring himself to incriminate Haigh. Kayser suggested that it was Strachan, not Haigh, who had taken part in the shooting of Wayne Smith, but Strachan denied it. Kayser also accused Strachan of having killed Brearley after she had repulsed his sexual advances. Again, Strachan denied the allegation.

When the trial moved on to the death of Eva Karlson, the court was told that all that was left by the time police recovered her remains was a hand, bone fragments, some clothing and jewellery. It was enough, however, for the crown to determine that she had been shot. Sergeant Leslie Charles Pont of the forensic science laboratory said he found the hand submerged in Mississippi Creek on 30 July 1979, the same day more grisly remains were found by the police search and rescue squad.

Squad Sergeant Andrew Russell then told of searching for spent cartridges near Mississippi Creek and coming across what appeared to be the remnants of a campsite. A single-bed mattress and a garbage dump were also found. A woman's blouse came to light, followed by the discovery of logs forming 'a sort of dam' in the creek. Entangled in the logs was a bra. 'I also noticed entangled in the logs some bones and some other fragments of clothing, or pieces of material,' Sergeant Russell said. He added that some hair and a locket were found beside the creek. Forensic experts were then called in. Sergeant Pont took up the story, saying that as well as the bones and a clump of hair, some skin was found near the creek. Beneath a cluster of small branches on the southern side of the creek, he found the hand — badly decomposed and with four rings on the fingers.

The jury of eight men and four women considered all the evidence very carefully before finding Quinn not guilty of the murder of Eva Karlson. They found Wright not guilty of the murders of Karlson and Brearley but guilty of the murders of Wayne Smith, Sheryle Gardner and Danny Mitchell. Haigh was found guilty of the murders of Wayne Smith, Sheryle Gardner, Danny Mitchell and Lisa Brearley. The failure to obtain any conviction on the Karlson murder charge was probably due to a lack both of scientific evidence and of witnesses other than Strachan, who the jury almost certainly regarded as unreliable.

For the murders of which they were convicted, Wright and Haigh were sentenced to life imprisonment, but it was not the end of their story. Two years after his conviction for four murders, Haigh, while in gaol, confessed to two more, both of which had taken place while he, Wright and Quinn were on their 1978–79 rampage. Haigh said that during the armed robbery of a Tattslotto agency, he shot a fifty-eight-year-old woman in the back of the head. Three months later, he said, he shot a forty-five-year-old father of two in the stomach during the robbery of a pizza parlour.

Then, in 1993, Haigh was given another life sentence, his seventh, for the murder of a fellow prisoner in a B Division cell at Pentridge. It was alleged that Haigh had helped the prisoner to commit suicide. The trial, before Mr Justice Coldrey, heard that Haigh helped Donald Hatherley, thirty-six, to hang himself by putting a noose around his neck, kicking a cupboard away from beneath him, then throwing his weight onto Hatherley's shoulders so the noose would strangle him. Representing himself in court, Haigh pleaded not guilty. He claimed that Hatherley was suicidal and he did no more than help him carry out his own wish to die.

Mr Justice Coldrey took a different view. 'You were ready and willing to utilise the death wish of an unstable and vulnerable man as a vehicle for self-fulfilment,' the trial judge said. In trying to explain to the jury why his helping Hatherley was not murder, Haigh told how he had held a knife to the throat of Lisa Brearley — so another man could rape her — before he stabbed her 157 times. 'To me, murder is when you have somebody wriggling under a bedspread when you're pointing a gun at their head ... or exhibiting some form of protest at meeting the Reaper,' he said dramatically. He failed to convince the jury of the difference and they convicted him.

Haigh then applied to the Supreme Court for a minimum sentence to be set for his seven life terms. At the request of the Director of Public Prosecutions, Mr Bernard Bongiorno QC, Mr Justice George Hampel adjourned the application for ten years. After that time, he said, Haigh could be given an overall non-parole term, following which he would be eligible for release.

Wright made headlines again in October 1987. As a protest after two prisoners suffering from AIDS were placed in cells near them in Jika Jika, Wright and four other notorious criminals started a fire. The fire quickly grew out of control and burned through wiring operating the electronically locked doors. Unable to escape, Wright and his companions died in the blaze. So Wright, like his volatile friend Quinn, died by fire in Pentridge. In October 1985 prisoner Alekos Taikmaskis, then thirty-seven, was sentenced to ten years for the manslaughter of Quinn. He had pleaded not guilty to murder, even though he had poured industrial glue over Quinn and thrown lighted matches at him.

Trial judge Mr Justice Tadgell said Taikmaskis had committed a criminal act of the gravest degree that showed a cruel disregard for a fellow human being. Evidence was given that Quinn had taunted Taikmaskis for some time about the rape of his former girlfriend. Justice Tadgell said the effect of the taunts had probably been heightened by a video screened for prisoners the night before the fiery attack on Quinn. The video had contained explicit sex scenes, including rape. Showing such material to prisoners was, in the judge's view, 'quite extraordinary'. Taikmaskis was already serving life for murder and twenty-two years on two counts of assault with intent to murder and armed robbery. Justice Tadgell ordered that the ten-year sentence be served concurrently and set no minimum term.

Fitting Wright and Haigh, as well as Quinn, into conventional tandem killer categories is not easy. All three were very much part of the criminal milieu and carried out most of the murders for what we called, at the beginning of this book, 'defensive' reasons — in other words, people were eliminated because they could identify the killers. At least some of the murders, however, were carried out with an enjoyment — a love of taking life, if you like — that does not seem to have been part of most defensive or professional tandem killings. In this sense, although the crimes of the three men were very different from those of the hedonistic killers we have examined elsewhere in this book, there is at least some similarity between their crimes and those of thrill killers.

Conclusion

Catching Tandem Killers

Throughout this book we have argued that most tandem killings cannot be explained by a simple theory of dominance–submission relationships between two people. In our view there is not enough evidence to support the proposition that one dominant personality overwhelms and controls a more submissive acquaintance, friend or lover, forcing them to participate in lethal violence. Clearly, when the characters of each of the tandem killers are analysed there is a strong argument to suggest that one of the killers is dominant and the other is submissive. But this is not the same as arguing that the less dominant person is simply a passive and almost robot-like follower of the violent fantasies and sick mind of the other.

In most of the hedonistic killings that we have looked at there are clear signs that the supposedly submissive partner initiated a great deal of the violence that was inflicted upon the hapless victim — and enjoyed doing it. In the Kingscliff murder, the adolescent victim was kicked so strongly by Luckman — the so-called submissive partner of the two killers — that the young murderer had to seek medical attention. Similar instances of 'submissive' partners initiating, without any duress, horrendous violence, can be seen in the case of Catherine and David Birnie, in the Watt and Beck murders, and in many of the other examples of sexual homicides that we have discussed in this book.

What is apparent in the psychological interplay between the two killers is the sheer enjoyment that each of the partners appears to experience in inflicting violence in the presence of the other person. The actual killing itself is also a way for the submissive accomplice to show his or her solidarity with the dominant partner — just as it provides the dominant killer with a means of demonstrating strength and power to the submissive partner. So, for example, Paul Luckman kicked his victim hard, as if to say to the more dominant Robin Reid 'I, too, share your fantasy and I, too, enjoy hurting this boy and I want to enjoy what you enjoy'. But Luckman was not acting out the shared fantasy just because he was afraid of the consequences of withdrawing from lustful violence. Rather, he was engaging in aggression because he enjoyed fulfilling a fantasy that he had nurtured and developed and shared with the older man for some time. In Luckman's and Reid's case, as well as in a significant number of the other cases we have looked at in this book, it is the sharing of an intense and deadly fantasy that distinguishes hedonistic killers from the other type of tandem murderers.

Tandem killers engage in torture and murder because they enjoy the emotions that such activity brings with it. The killers require their victims to be anonymous props on whom they can inflict their lethal desires. These desires might be based on one or a combination of sexual thrills, the pursuit of power over another human being, or the sharing of a fantasy with the person they are infatuated with, but they are all emotions that give them intense pleasure. In our analysis of tandem killings we have been struck by how much the pursuit of the ultimate sexual orgasm becomes the driving force for at least one of the two offenders. But the orgasm may not necessarily involve actual intercourse or even overtly sexual acts. It is, instead, the shared sexual fantasy itself that propels the offenders to commit their evil deeds.

David Birnie, for example, was always seeking new ways of fulfilling an essentially voracious sexual craving. Sexual penetration with his victims did not always occur, but the torturing of his young female victims became part of his ritual in his attempt to maximise his sexual experience. Indeed, in Birnie's search for the ultimate orgasmic occurrence, it seems that the capture and killing of the women themselves gave him the greatest pleasure. The actual murder was, for Birnie, an integral part of the sexual turn-on, just as it was for other tandem killers. Christopher Lowery, for example told his partner Charles King that 'it would be good to see [Rosalyn Nolte] die'.

Hedonistic murder offers the participants a range of feelings and emotions that are not dissimilar to those experienced by sportsmen and women. We have been struck by the number of times tandem killers talk about experiencing a 'high' or are 'elated' as they first capture and then rape, torture and finally kill their victims. Hunting humans, in other words, becomes a compelling activity for those who engage in it just as rugby league or the love of vintage cars or any other hobby becomes compelling and satisfying for many devotees of these activities.

Of course, in tandem killings there is always a great deal of pathology involved that is not present among most of the participants in body sports. The slow and deliberate murder of another human being is, by definition, always pathological, although this is not the same as saying that the killer or killers suffer a mental illness. In our view the vast majority of tandem murderers know exactly what they are doing when they decide to engage in lethal violence and, in most cases, have carefully planned the mayhem they indulge in. There is no dissociation, loss of control or 'defect of reason' that characterises those commonly acquitted of murder on the grounds of insanity.

While in psychiatric terms tandem killers might not be generally described as mentally ill, in most cases they can be classified as psychopaths with a particular paraphilia — that is, a recurrent and intense sexual urge that involves the suffering and humiliation of non-consenting victims. And the word 'psychopath', although often abused in both the professional and popular literature, is a relevant term to use with most of our tandem killers. Psychopaths typically show signs of self-importance and extreme self-centredness.

Robert Simon, author of the important book on psychopathic killers entitled *Bad Men Do What Good Men Dream*, cogently argues that the two fundamental distinguishing characteristics of psychopaths are their inability to feel ordinary human empathy and affection for others, and the perpetrating of repeated antisocial acts. 'Psychopaths can have lustful sex,' he says. 'But for them the experience is devoid of any intimacy or commitment — the partner is essentially an instrument.' How well this describes most of the tandem killers examined in this book. Crump and Baker saw Virginia Morse as nothing more than a plaything on which the two killers projected their own murderous desires. So, too, did Watt and Beck with twelve-year-old Sian Kingi; and Lowery and King with fifteen-year-old Roslyn Nolte.

Tandem sexual killers appear to have had the same disturbed and fragmented childhoods that characterise lone serial sexual offenders. Experts do not know precisely what it is about these childhoods that triggers their later lethal life — indeed, some researchers argue that such killers are born that way while others argue that they develop into murderers through their teens and young adulthood. Either way, a troubled childhood only inflates their inherited psychopathic tendencies. But it is often this very psychopathology in the tandem killers' actions that reveals important characteristics underlying their psyche. The bizarre slashing, slow strangulation or mutilation of a victim acts very much like other physical evidence in signalling the sort of person or persons who commit such atrocious murders.

In their recent book on the Backpacker murders, *Sins of the Brother*, Mark Whittaker and Les Kennedy describe how Richard Basham, an anthropologist who assisted police in profiling the case, believed that two killers, rather than one, were involved in the Backpacker murders. Basham was struck by the fact that in at least some of the murders the victims were separated from each other before they were murdered. The anthropologist considered that this might have been done because the perpetrator was too embarrassed to perform his well-rehearsed fantasy in front of the other victim. Much more likely, however, was the possibility that two people were involved in the killings and that one of them did not want to act out his gruesome fantasy in front of the other.

The decapitation of one of the victims also suggested to Basham that two killers were involved and that one of the killers was making a statement to his submissive partner. That statement was 'I'm the crazy motherfucker around here and this decapitated body is proof of that.' Whittaker and Kennedy recount how Basham believed that this was domination of both the victim and the more submissive partner, and that it was probably a sign of a killer who had had an overbearing and brutal father. Although only one person has been convicted of the Backpacker murders, there is considerable evidence — presented in the Whittaker and Kennedy book — that another person was involved. Both the circumstances surrounding the abductions of the victims and the way in which they were disposed of adds credence to this view.

Profiling hedonistic crimes may well have value over and above providing insights into the personality characteristics of the killer or killers. The way in which the victims were killed and the crime scene itself, for example, have long been used by FBI profilers as useful indicators of who the offender or offenders were. For example, FBI-trained investigators have noted that in some sexual homicides, a crime scene has characteristics that they call organised or disorganised in nature. These indices tell us much about the level of planning and premeditation (including the build-up of fantasy associated with the murder) exhibited by the killer or killers. In an organised crime scene, the way the victim was killed and the overall *modus operandi* of the killer reflect a methodical, well-organised offender who takes great care not to leave any physical evidence behind. On the other hand, a disorganised crime scene is one where spontaneity and a lack of planning characterise the murder and where there is little or no attempt to hide any incriminating evidence.

In many tandem murders the crime scene reflects aspects of both organised and disorganised characteristics because more than one offender is involved. For that reason different personalities are reflected in the way the victim is killed and the method by which the body is disposed of. For instance, although Reid and Luckman fantasised about killing a young boy for many years, it was apparent that the actual crime they committed was more a result of a chance meeting of suitable victims (two adolescent youths hitchhiking) and motivated offenders (Reid and Luckman). The fact that the body was only buried in a shallow grave and that one of the boys was able to talk himself into being released also indicates a crime that had both organised and disorganised characteristics.

Profiling is based on the premise that anyone who leaves a crime scene takes something from the scene and leaves something of himself behind. Although the technique is mainly used in the case of serial offenders — offenders who kill more than twice — it also has applications in some tandem murders, although it has rarely been used in the Australian cases profiled in this book.

Profiling is, however, slowly beginning to be accepted by Australian law enforcement officials, so it may have an important role to play in the future. When conventional investigative methods have failed, profiling can have real benefits. The reason for this is that when motives — traditionally used by law enforcement agencies to investigate killings — fail to identify a suspect, then new leads on why a crime was committed and who may be responsible can be generated by profiling techniques. We must remember, though, that, contrary to popular fiction, profiling does not immediately provide investigators with the name, address and shoe size of the offender. Its most valuable role is in significantly reducing the pool of potential suspects and allowing law enforcement officers to narrow their investigations to a more specific focus.

An issue that generates much public discussion is what should happen to tandem killers once they are caught. We do not wish to cover the relative advantages and disadvantages of the death penalty in this book, except to say that we see no merit in reintroducing into this country a long disbanded and discredited punishment method. As, respectively, a journalist and a criminologist, we have both seen too many miscarriages of justice to lend our support to the ultimate penalty that society can inflict on the criminal. But the death penalty is an emotive issue and, while we agree in principle that it fails to act as a deterrent to murder, some conflict between us remains. The criminologist believes that a civilised society should not engage in the barbarous practice of legal murder no matter how horrendous the crime that may have been committed by the convicted killer(s). The journalist, however, while agreeing that a civilised society should not have to resort to capital punishment, still feels there are times when it might be justified, particularly in the case of those preying upon innocent children, but only when guilt is established beyond all doubt.

Neither of us however, are, convinced, as civil

libertarians or penal reformers would have us believe, that every person has the capacity to change their behaviour and that most killers can safely be released back into the community. It may be that some of our non-hedonistic tandem killers — Harold Peckman, for example — deserves to be discharged back into society after serving a lengthy prison sentence. But this is not the case with most of the offenders we have surveyed here. In our view the tandem killer's character is so firmly formed that it carves out the destiny of that killer for almost all his or her whole life. Although, when they are due for parole, many tandem killers say they have changed for the better, we have seen little evidence in the scientific literature to suggest that significant changes might have taken place.

When we have questioned experienced prison professionals about the lives and behaviour of the killers while in prison, we have been struck by how many of these professionals say that the killers have maintained their basic personality structure. They may have become more manipulative and cunning while in prison and the strength of their murderous fantasies could well have declined, but underneath the surface the same lethal impulses remain. In short, their essential personality traits and their propensity towards violence continues unabated.

Psychiatrists and psychologists admit they have little to offer these offenders by way of treatment or rehabilitation programs. As Robert Simon puts it: 'despite valiant efforts, the treatment of antisocial personalities has been an abysmal failure'. For tandem killers are men, and women too, who have deliberately chosen to commit themselves to the grossest forms of evil. Their commitment to this lifestyle is one that is hardly likely to change during the passage of time, either in or outside prison. They should, therefore, remain inside prison for most — if not all — of their natural lives as rare but visible symbols of the ultimate corruption of the human psyche.

Bibliography

Adler, Freda. (1975) *Sisters in Crime*, McGraw-Hill, New York.

Britton, Paul. Quoted in *The Australian*, 27 November 1995.

Broomfield, N. (1992) *Aileen Wuornos: The Selling of a Serial Killer*, Orion Home Video, Los Angeles.

Brown, M. (1998) *Australian Crime: Chilling Tales of Our Time*, Lansdowne, Sydney 1993.

Green, E. (1993) *The Intent to Kill: Making Sense of Murder*, Clevedon Books, Baltimore.

Kidd, P. (1993) *Never To Be Released*, Pan Macmillan, Sydney.

Maslaw, Abraham. (1998) *Towards a Psychology of Being*, edited by Richard Lowry, 3rd edition, John Wiley, New York.

Masters, B. (1997) *She Must Have Known*, Transworld Publishers, London.

Mykyta, A.M. (1981) *It's a Long Way to Truro*, McPhee Gribble, Melbourne.

Simon, R. (1996) *Bad Men Do What Good Men Dream*, American Psychiatric Press, Washington DC.

Waters, D. and D. Lane (1998) *Raging Waters*, Macmillan, Sydney.

West, Don. (1983) 'Sex offences and offending', in *Crime and justice: an annual review of research*, edited by M. Tonry & N. Morris, vol 5, University of Chicago

Press, Chicago.

Whittaker, M. and L. Kennedy (1998) *Sins of the Brother*, Macmillan, Sydney.

Wilson, C. and P. Pitman (1984) *Encyclopaedia of Murder*, Pan Books, London.

Wilson, P. (1985) *Murder of the Innocents*, Rigby, Adelaide.

Wilson, P. (1998) *Black Death White Hands*, (second impression) Allen & Unwin, Sydney.

www.ingramcontent.com/pod-product-compliance
Lightning Source LLC
Chambersburg PA
CBHW022053290426
44109CB00014B/1083